THE COUNSELLING RELATIONSHIP

Susan Oldfield **THE COUNSELLING RELATIONSHIP**

A study of the client's experience

Routledge & Kegan Paul

London, Boston, Melbourne and Henley

First published in 1983
by Routledge & Kegan Paul plc
39 Store Street, London WC1E 7DD,
9 Park Street, Boston, Mass. 02108, USA,
296 Beaconsfield Parade, Middle Park,
Melbourne, 3206, Australia, and
Broadway House, Newtown Road,
Henley-on-Thames, Oxon RG9 1EN
Set in Press Roman 10pt by
Cambrian Typesetters, Farnborough
and printed in Great Britain by
Billing & Sons Ltd
Worcester

Library of Congress Cataloging in Publication Data

Oldfield, Susan, 1943–

The counselling relationship.
Bibliography: p.
Includes index.
1. Isis Centre. 2. Counseling – England.
3. Mental health services – England. I. Title.
DNLM: 1. Counseling. 2. Professional-patient
relations. WM 55 044c
RA790.7.G70'43 1983   362.2'2'0942574   83-2902

ISBN 0-7100-9422-1

to Martin

Contents

Tables

Foreword

It is generally accepted that, in this country, somewhere between a quarter and a third of people who consult their family doctor are suffering from emotional problems rather than from physical disease. During the past thirty years, an increasing number of general practitioners have become interested in, and accomplished at dealing with, emotional difficulties. Many have sought special training for themselves at centres like the Tavistock Institute of Human Relations, or have attached to their practices skilled social workers to act as counsellors. But some doctors still consider that treating anything other than physical disease is outside their province, and regard the prescription of a tranquilliser as all that is required. It is hard to blame them. In a busy surgery, where six minutes or less is all that is available for each patient, the doctor often has neither the time nor the patience to offer that dedicated, listening ear which is the essential prerequisite for comprehending and alleviating emotional problems.

It can be argued that these patients should be referred to the psychiatrist. Only a tiny proportion are so referred, for two reasons. The first is that provision for out-patient psychotherapy is woefully inadequate. Most psychiatrists are overworked, and so, in most parts of the country, it is only the severer forms of mental illness which are sent to them. The second is that many people suffering from emotional distress do not want to be labelled as psychiatric patients and referred to clinics for the mentally ill. In this they have the support of many thoughtful people, including the psychiatrist Thomas Szasz, who question whether the 'problems in living' which cause so much distress, should properly be defined as 'illness' in the sense in which physical disease is so regarded.

The prevalence of emotional problems can, in part, be attributed to the defects of Western culture. We have replaced the extended family with the nuclear family, so that each individual has far fewer people

to whom he may naturally turn when troubled than he does in less
'advanced' cultures. Moreover, in these days of frequent divorce, even
the nuclear family does not necessarily cohere, and is itself the source
of emotional conflict. In addition, a high proportion of the population
live in large cities rather than in villages. In the latter, it is impossible
not to have neighbours who, although they may gossip, will also
provide support in times of trouble. In the city, a human being may live
for years in a bed-sitting room without knowing who lives in the rest
of the house, let alone the street. Nothing is so alienating as life in a
large city; and people who live in one often begin by feeling cut off
from others and end by being cut off from themselves.

The decline of religious belief is also an important factor. Those with
faith are not protected against the emotional storms which afflict us all,
but may be helped to weather them by the conviction that there is a
God who cares, whose help can be enlisted through prayer. In addition,
they may be able to rely on the support of their own congregation and
its ministers.

For many distressed people, virtually none of the resources referred
to are available. It was to meet their needs that the Isis Centre was
opened in 1970. In this book, Susan Oldfield tells the story of its
inception and of its gradual establishment as an important feature of
life in Oxford. Throughout its existence, the type of client seeking help,
the kind of problems dealt with, and the results of counselling have all
been carefully monitored. No one can help all of the people all of the
time, and failures have not been glossed over. But it cannot be doubted
that the Isis Centre has been, and is, a signal success. In this book, we
have the clients' own words to confirm this. Over and over again we
read such sentences as: 'I have begun to find out how I want to live.'
'I don't get into that feeling of total isolation and depression.' Positive
results can often be achieved after only a few counselling sessions; in
some cases, after only one. Anyone who still believes that substantial
alleviation of emotional problems requires years of psychoanalysis
should read this book, which will convince him otherwise. A skilled
counsellor — and he or she must be properly trained - can often
achieve substantial and permanent alleviation quickly, although there
will always be clients who require extended therapy. It must be
emphasised that the counsellor's task is first to clarify the problem, and
then to aid the client in finding his own solution. Anyone can proffer
tea and sympathy: professionals know that only helping the client to
help himself is likely to be effective.

It goes without saying that general practitioners, psychiatrists, social
workers, probation officers, and many other professionals in the
medical and social services will want to read this book. I also strongly
commend it to administrators, both at the local level and in the central
offices of the Department of Health and Social Security. The Isis

Centre is not an expensive resource. In terms of the results achieved, and of the load lifted both from the surgeries of general practitioners and from the hospital services, it is extremely cheap. This kind of centre can help to cut the enormous drug bill of the National Health Service, by rendering the prescription of tranquillisers less necessary. Complex operations and elaborate gadgetry possess a dramatic appeal which ensures them more funding than they sometimes deserve. It is vital that those in charge of the National Health Service come to realise the importance of setting up and supporting centres similar to the Isis Centre throughout the country. Susan Oldfield's book points the way to a future which must come.

Anthony Storr, F.R.C.P., F.R.C.Psych.

Acknowledgments

First of all, I would like to thank all the clients who participated in this study, and who helped us to understand the nature of their experience in counselling. I am very grateful for their generosity in conveying their thoughts and feelings with such vividness and immediacy. Their contributions, while completely anonymous, provide the invaluable dimension of personal experience for our exploration of the counselling process. Every effort has been made to ensure that neither they, nor other clients to whom reference is made, will be individually recognisable in any way.

Thanks are also due to the members of the counselling team who took part in the study, and who made possible the collection of these portraits of a variety of counselling contacts. The work of twelve counsellors was involved, and I am grateful for their care and patience in reflecting upon it.

The Isis Centre as a whole owes gratitude to Dr Bertram Mandelbrote, for his original vision, and for his guidance in its early years. This work has been sustained and extended by the Centre's present consultant, Dr Peter Agulnik. Much is due to his commitment to developing an organisation which can steadily offer thinking and understanding in response to many kinds of anxiety and distress. Valuable support has also been offered to the Centre throughout its life by Miss Betty Gormley, to whom we are grateful.

The deepest debt, however, is owed to Mrs Pauline Holroyd, who was the co-ordinator of the Isis Centre for the first ten years. She established and built it up with immense patience and devoted energy. Her conviction that troubled people are entitled to serious, sensitive attention, and her confidence in their capacity to understand and take responsibility for themselves, formed the twin principles on which the Centre is founded. I would like to express my personal gratitude for her teaching and her example.

Acknowledgments

My thanks are due to many people for help in the detailed work of the study itself: to Mrs Pauline Holroyd, for assistance in its design and for interviewing some of the clients; to Miss Jenny Biggar, for much help with collecting the data, and for typing the manuscript; to Mrs Annie Davies and Mrs Penny Bowen for further preparation of the typed material; and to those who read the manuscript and gave me many helpful suggestions. In particular, I would like to thank Dr Anthony Storr for his help and encouragement at all stages of the project.

I am grateful to the Oxfordshire Area Health Authority Research Committee for funding the study initially, and for providing further support as it developed, and, finally, to the author's literary estate and The Hogarth Press Ltd. for permission to quote from *Psychoanalytic Theory, Therapy and the Self* by Harry Guntrip (1971).

Chapter 1

The origins of the Isis Centre

Some discouragement, some faintness of heart at the new real future which replaces the imaginary is not unusual, and we do not expect people to be deeply moved by what is not unusual. That element of tragedy which lies in the very fact of frequency has not yet wrought itself into the coarse emotion of mankind; and perhaps our frames could hardly bear much of it. If we had a keen vision and feeling of all ordinary human life, it would be like hearing the grass grow and the squirrel's heart beat, and we should die of that roar that lies on the other side of silence. As it is, the quickest of us walk about well wadded with stupidity.   (George Eliot, *Middlemarch*)

It is with 'that element of tragedy which lies in the very fact of frequency' that this book is concerned: with the kinds of unhappiness, perplexity and discouragement that form part of 'all ordinary human life'. George Eliot is describing the sinking feelings of a young wife as she slowly apprehends the real nature of the marriage on which she has just embarked. There is a dreary contrast between this and the ideal relationship she had hitherto imagined. We all embark on new stages in our lives with some unrealistic hopes and some unfounded fears, and we take time to grasp and cope with the realities as they unfold. At such times we are particularly vulnerable, while we are unsure whether we have the resources to deal with the unfamiliar demands of the new situation. A young man leaving his parents' home for the first time; a mother holding her small baby; someone embarking on an unfamiliar and responsible job; people letting go of their working roles and preparing for retirement: at each stage we experience trepidation as well as excitement, anxiety as well as hope.

At such times of transition we are also liable to encounter confusing shadows of earlier experiences. A new, authoritative boss may awaken daunting memories of a tyrannical schoolmaster, or a stern father, and so rouse old feelings of childishness and rage. A wife, in the intimacy of

1

a newly established home, may seem more and more to resemble an elusive or an overwhelming mother, and her husband may be hard put to develop an adult relationship that is not jeopardised by feelings which remain, still unresolved, from his childhood.

At times of major changes in our lives, we often become aware of anxieties and difficulties that, in fact, we experience less dramatically all the time. As we live we accumulate ideas that seem to make sense of our experience. Some of these may be accurate perceptions; others have a protective function, interpreting difficult realities in a way that makes them more bearable. Such distortions may serve us well as a temporary defence but they grow misleading and restrictive as our situation changes. If a child, for example, has to deal with an environment which is often frightening and unpredictable, he will be forced to adopt defensive strategies which allow him to survive. As he grows up and the external environment offers new possibilities, he may be locked by his earlier, necessary tactics into a position that he cannot easily change. If he has survived once by, for example, withholding trust and refusing to care, he will find it very hard to respond differently, even when it would be safe to do so and the satisfying development of his life requires it. We have all been children, and we are all liable to the resurgence of anxieties associated with being small and relatively helpless. Such fearfulness, and the defensive measures adopted to deal with it, tangle with our adult hopes and purposes, sometimes bringing us to a standstill.

Confused feelings of this kind are often hard for a person to sort out for himself. He retreats instead into further defensive systems in order to escape from the mental pain they cause. Disproportionate anxiety or inexplicable depression may add themselves to the existing difficulties. Such feelings are the more intolerable because they appear to the sufferer to be, to some degree, incomprehensible. They do not seem to be, and indeed are not, accountable in terms simply of the immediate problems, and skilled help may be needed in finding their roots and easing the underlying conflicts.

In this book I shall describe a resource which offers help of this kind to people who find themselves in such painful and perplexing situations. It offers an alternative to the existing possibilities of treatment within a medical or psychiatric setting, or of private therapy, which is both scarce and expensive. Firstly, however, let us consider some of the ways in which people usually attempt to deal with their problems, for, of course, in the majority of instances, no professional help is either offered or sought.

Common forms of problem-solving

We are all familiar with moods of anxiety and depression, varying in intensity and duration according to a complicated web of circumstances. If a person has sufficient previous experience of eventually emerging from such feelings, and of surmounting difficulties, he can tolerate them without being overwhelmed. In time he finds the energy to solve the new problems or to survive the pain of a particular disappointment or loss. If this store of confidence and experience proves inadequate to meet the current trouble, he may have trusted family or friends to whom he may turn, who can temporarily support him until his own courage and hope return. Uncritical support from people close to us serves not only to augment our strength with theirs, but also, in the longer term, to liberate our own resources and restore our confidence in them.

We commonly meet stressful situations with such stores of resources, both internal and external, on which we can draw to meet our needs. Severe additional strains, however, are encountered when both these sources of strength fail. That is, when the new demand, by its severity, or simply as the last straw on an accumulating load of stress, exceeds our skill, courage and understanding; and when those about us are, or seem, unable or unwilling to help us. The resultant feelings of helplessness and despair, rooted as they are in childhood experiences of being small, lost and ineffectual, loom very large, and further reduce our capacity for dealing with the situation.

That people do experience such high levels of distress very frequently, and that their reactions may become established as destructive patterns of self-doubt, inadequacy or illness, is well documented. Surveys which seek to assess the prevalence of emotional disturbance in the community are in accord in finding large numbers of people who are seriously anxious or depressed. Many are troubled to a degree which impairs their ability to work, to relate to others and to cope with their everyday lives (Taylor and Chave, 1964; Wing and Hailey, 1972; Brown and Harris, 1978). Such unhappiness takes a variety of forms. They range from the common experiences of tension, crying and feeling exhausted and despairing, through various kinds of neurotic symptoms, to behaviour and experiences which raise frightening thoughts of madness.

Finding themselves unable to cope with emotional and practical difficulties in their lives, people often turn to those near them, and sometimes receive constructive help. Brown and Harris (1978), in their study of women in a London borough, found that the existence of even one close relationship, which allowed a woman to confide her problems and express her feelings, was an effective protector against overwhelming depression. Many people, however, as an intrinsic part of their problems, fail to make relationships of that quality; others are simply a long way from those who might otherwise be confidants. Furthermore, the very nature of depressing feelings may make a person reluctant to confide in anyone else: his self-esteem is so low that he doubts if he is worth that much attention, or he is unhopeful about the response he may receive.

In reporting a study of people who sought help from the Family Welfare Association, Mayer and Timms (1970) considered the reasons that clients gave for not relying more on their informal network of friends and family. In some cases people proved to be isolated by distance from those to whom they might have talked. Perhaps they had moved recently, or come to a new locality on getting married, and had as yet made no new friends. For those who did have people near them to whom they might have turned, other barriers existed. Social norms as to what could be openly discussed without embarrassment or shame tended to inhibit them. They also felt that it might be an imposition on others to burden them with worries and upsetting problems. Other people hesitated because they were unsure whether such disclosures would be treated as confidential. Of those who had tried to talk things over with friends, neighbours or relatives, some had been disappointed or further confused by unacceptable, conflicting or ineffectual advice.

Because the informal network of support often seems inadequate or inappropriate, many people suffering from emotional stress seek some form of professional help. Most usually they turn to their family doctors. Various estimates have been made as to how large a proportion of a general practitioner's caseload is composed of people bringing problems which are primarily emotional in nature. Although the precise numbers vary, the consensus is that they are substantial, in some reports even approaching 30 per cent (Shepherd, Cooper, Brown and Kalton, 1966; Cooper, Fry and Kalton, 1969; Goldberg and Blackwell, 1970). This represents a heavy burden on the doctor's time, and accounts for the widespread prescription of tranquillising and anti-depressant drugs. Only a very small proportion of people who seek help from their doctors in anxiety about their emotional states is referred for specialist psychiatric treatment (Wing and Wing, 1970; Bransby, 1974). Goldberg and Huxley (1980) report a prevalence rate of emotional distress, which meets their criteria for psychiatric disorder, of 250 per thousand at risk per year. Of these, 230 cases may reach family doctors, but only 140 are likely to be recognised as psychological in nature, and only seventeen will be referred for specialist psychiatric care.

Goldberg and Huxley have made a very careful survey, both of the available data concerning the prevalence of mental distress in the community, and of the pathways taken, or not taken, to professional help. They analyse the complex 'filters' of personal, social and medical decision-making processes which operate at each stage of a person's movement towards help. Their findings confirm the widespread occurrence of severe degrees of anxiety and depression in the community, and the fact that it is likely that men and women suffering in these ways will at some time approach their family doctors. It is found that people who are lonely are particularly likely to do so, in contrast with those with close and secure networks of family and friends. Many variables enter at this stage, in addition to those which relate directly to the individual and his or her problem, and these factors strongly affect the outcome. For example, women are found to be more likely than men to experience incapacitating kinds of distress, and also to be more likely to consult their doctors; furthermore, general practitioners more readily define difficulties that are presented by women as emotional in nature. Nevertheless, they are found to be less likely to refer women than men for specialist help, and more likely to prescribe for them sedatives, tranquillisers or anti-depressants.

Even if they themselves recognise that their problems are emotional or social in origin, most people present them to their general practitioner in the form of physical symptoms. Goldberg and Huxley review the evidence that doctors vary greatly in their readiness to take such presentations at face value, or their willingness to explore further and to hear an underlying appeal for help of a psychological kind. Should they do so, serious questions are raised even then about the nature and quality of the treatment that is usually offered, particularly in as far as it is likely to depend heavily on psychotropic drugs, often inappropriately prescribed in the first instance and repeated without further interviews.

General practitioners vary widely also in their interest and skill in relation to emotional disorders, and in the degree to which they see their role as a counselling or psychotherapeutic one. Much attention has been paid to the quality of the doctor-patient relationship and the ways in which this can be enhanced (Balint, 1964), but even at its most sensitive it is limited by the restrictions of available time. Balint and Norell (1973) emphasise this fact in the title of their book: *Six Minutes for the Patient*.

There are, however, more fundamental factors which make it questionable that the doctor's surgery is the most appropriate setting for people seeking ways of coping more effectively with emotional problems. Traditionally the patient brings his physical complaints to the doctor and trusts to his expertise in diagnosis and prescription. The patient's role is mainly a passive one, that of submitting to the doctor's instructions, in the expectation that the cure will be effected without much more effort on his own part than that of obedience. This legitimised relief from responsibility is one of the privileges of the sick role in our culture (Mechanic, 1968). When, however, the distress for which the person seeks help is of a psychological rather than a physical nature, it may be argued that the initial assumption of the sick role, and the passive expectation that someone else will offer a 'cure', are further steps away from mental health.

It is an important paradox that the person who is struggling with unsatisfactory relationships, who is failing to cope with everyday problems in living, and who feels confused and despairing, needs a kind of help which in no way undermines his sense of being responsible for himself. Many distressed people recognise this but are perplexed as to where to seek it. They may have approached their doctors, perhaps even producing a physical symptom to make this both feel and seem appropriate, but they are discouraged and disappointed by the lack of time available for talking, and maybe by a repeat prescription for pills in which they no longer have any faith. Where else can they turn?

Studies in Oxfordshire

It was in response to such considerations that the project to be described here was originally formulated. In the 1960s, to assist in planning the development of psychiatric services in Oxfordshire, two community studies were undertaken. Their purpose was to identify and assess the dimensions of the psychiatric needs of the local population, and then to consider how they might best be met. The findings of this research were in accord with those of similar studies of other regions. That is, that psychosis was rare; that neurotic symptomatology was widespread and largely untreated; and that incapacitating degrees of anxiety and depression were distressingly common (Monro, 1965). Follow-up studies in the same localities were conducted five years later. In many instances, individuals who had been suffering from distressing moods or symptoms at the time of the original investigation were now free of them, yet levels of neurotic disturbance were much the same over all. This seemed to be explained in part by the emergence of neurotic reactions in other members of the same households. The hopeful evidence of spontaneous remission of symptoms, or their adequate treatment by existing resources, was qualified by signs that family stress might now merely be concentrated in another member. The role of the troubled or disturbed person had perhaps been re-allocated rather than rendered unnecessary.

The sheer quantity of distress revealed by these studies made it clear that existing psychiatric and medical resources could not possibly attend to it directly, even if this were desirable or appropriate. But if a new National Health Service resource were to be developed, with the aim of preventing or reducing some of this suffering, what characteristics should it have?

It was felt that one important function would be to support and enhance the work of existing agencies, both professional and voluntary, without duplicating any of their services. Clearly much of the load already fell on social workers, health visitors, probation officers, teachers, ministers, and other community workers. Valuable roles were

6

also played by organisations such as the Samaritans, and the Marriage Guidance Council, and by counsellors working in schools and colleges. If a community mental health centre were to be established, it was felt that it should develop, as one of its contributions, a consultation service, for the support and further training of those already involved in a variety of caring roles. It would also provide an information service for the public, as a guide to other specialised agencies.

There then remained the question of what might be offered directly to people who were searching for some help with the problems in living which they encountered and could not solve alone. The essential part was to devise a service which would add a new dimension to what was already available, and which would offer a valid alternative to the medical model which was not necessarily always appropriate. Another important capacity would be to respond to need, and to the approaches made to the centre as it became known locally, rather than to insist too rigidly on a preconceived plan.

The idea gradually clarified of a direct access counselling service, available for people to make their own approach, without the necessity of a medical referral. It would be designed to respond to a wide range of emotional problems, and would not be identified with a medical setting, either geographically or in the style of its work. Its aims would be to provide skilled psychological care for those people who conceived of themselves as distressed rather than ill, and who wanted to work on their problems without surrendering responsibility for themselves. The validity, or lack of it, of such an aim, and the accuracy with which it met a real community need, would be demonstrated gradually by the use made of it, and by its results.

The evolution of the Isis Centre

In later chapters I shall try to convey the nature of the therapeutic work of the Isis Centre. I would like first to outline its history, from its opening in 1970 to the present day.

The realisation of the ideas described in the previous section was initiated by a consultant psychiatrist, Dr Bertram Mandelbrote, from Littlemore Hospital in Oxford. He was interested in the extension of the psychiatric service into the community in various forms, including the establishment of group homes, the attachment of community psychiatric nurses to health centres, and other links with doctors in general practice. With the financial support of the Oxford Regional Health Authority, he planned a community mental health project, to be called the Isis Centre. Dr Leonard Elmhirst, of the Dartington Hall Trust, gave support to the idea, and provided premises for rental in the centre of Oxford. These have the advantages of being easily accessible, of having a 'shop-front' on to the street, and of being in keeping with the informal, approachable atmosphere that was intended. The accommodation is quite limited: it consists of a waiting-room, with an adjoining office for the receptionist; three counselling rooms, and one larger one, which is suitable for group meetings, but can also be used for individual or marital work. The premises were leased to what was then the Regional Hospital Board, and the day-to-day running was the responsibility of the Isis Group Hospital Management Committee.

The Centre opened in October, 1970. It had then only one full-time member of staff, Pauline Holroyd, the co-ordinator. Dr Peter Agulnik, a psychiatrist, also from Littlemore Hospital, was much concerned with the development of the service, and later become the consultant primarily responsible for the project. The plan, when the Centre opened, was for various members of hospital staff — for example, a social worker, the hospital chaplain, and members of the nursing staff — to make their skills as counsellors available in this new setting, for a regular part of their working time. Each of those who were interested, and who were prepared to study and develop the relevant skills, undertook to be regularly at the Isis Centre for perhaps a day or half a day a week. By the end of the first year a succession of counsellors was available to cover the hours when the Centre was open.

Voluntary help was also offered at this time by various groups, including students from the College of Further Education and from local theological colleges. Their particular interest was in running informal groups in the evenings, when the Centre would be open to provide companionship and shelter for people who were free to drop in at will. A volunteer undertook to open the Centre each night and to participate in the group that spontaneously formed.

Since one of the intentions of the project was to respond to the needs of the community, rather than offer it a fully preconceived service, the identity of the Isis Centre was deliberately kept flexible. At the beginning its doors were simply opened to see who would come. Also, meetings were held with a variety of professional and voluntary groups, to make the existence of the Centre known and to begin to clarify needs and potential roles. At this time, the possibility that it might develop with an emphasis on providing support for lonely, homeless and deprived people in the city was not ruled out. Alternatively, it might emerge that a more structured counselling service would be its primary role, or that these things would proceed together. The smallness of the premises, however, and their internal layout, seemed likely to lend themselves more readily to individual and small group work.

During the first year a part-time receptionist was allocated to the Centre, and this soon became a full-time post. Meanwhile the counselling team was gradually establishing its identity. It met regularly for four hours each week, for discussion of problems arising in the work, for further theoretical training, and for the experiential study of group dynamics. Close links were maintained at all times with other parts of the hospital structure, particularly with the Ashhurst and Ley Clinics, which provide day-care facilities, group work, and treatment for drug and alcohol problems. After about two years the demand for skilled counselling was such that the need was felt for some further members of staff. Their commitment would be primarily to the Isis Centre, as opposed to being shared with other hospital departments. Due to financial restrictions, it was a further two years before these appointments could be made, but then two part-time counselling posts were filled.

By this time, 1974, the main characteristics of the service provided by the Isis Centre were fairly well established: that is, a consultation and information service, and the provision of individual or group therapy to members of the public who made their own approach. Concurrently, an interest was strengthening in studying the counselling work as it proceeded, and in trying both to define its principal elements and to increase its effectiveness. This effort, supported by a series of research grants from the Area and Regional Health Authorities, has remained an important part of Isis Centre work. The more informal provision of support, in the form of the evening 'drop-in' groups, had gradually diminished, and ceased completely, soon after this time.

The consultation aspect of the work of the Isis Centre began to develop early, and it has remained a consistent part of the service. Other professional people have come, as individuals or in groups, to discuss, with a member of the Isis Centre team, problems arising in their own settings. Representatives of voluntary groups have also made use of this service. Approaches have been made by, for example, groups of teachers or health visitors; and by people offering specialised counselling services, such as those for students, for the bereaved, or for those with problems associated with homosexuality. The consultation may take the form of a single meeting, or of a limited number of sessions devoted to discussion of a specific problem; or of on-going meetings for more general exploration of the problems that occur within a particular agency. This is regarded as an important aspect of the work of the Centre, and it is intended that it should continue to expand.

Over the years the basic counselling team has grown, and it is also extended by people in training or working elsewhere (e.g. social workers, psychiatrists, psychologists), who seek experience of counselling in this setting. Because the team members change from time to time, and because there are alterations in needs and interests, both within and outside the Isis Centre, there are, of course, variations in organisation, training opportunities and support structures. In 1980, the counselling team had twelve members, who included two psychologists, three psychiatrists in training, two social workers, a nursing officer, a hospital chaplain, two counsellors with training and experience in marital work and one with a background in educational counselling and research. The back-up team consists of the psychiatrist who has consultant responsibility for the Centre, and the senior psychiatric social worker to the hospital service. Both have particular interest and experience in analytic psychotherapy. The team meets once a week for two hours, dividing into two small groups for part of this time, for the discussion of new cases, and meeting as a whole for the remaining time. Attendance at this meeting is a basic condition of joining the team. In addition, it is usual for each counsellor to arrange personal supervision for his work. Further opportunities for learning are provided by: a weekly study group, shared with members of the Ashhurst Clinic, for the purpose of increasing personal awareness, as it relates to the therapeutic task; and a weekly workshop in which a small group of counsellors share and study the development of ongoing cases. In addition, several members of the team are in personal therapy or analysis, or are involved in further training within institutions such as the Tavistock Institute of Human Relations or the Institute of Group Analysis.

This book is concerned with the counselling and psychotherapy aspects of the work of the Isis Centre. Its aim is to describe the style of therapeutic work that has evolved in this setting, as a result of an interactive process. This has involved the existing skills of the counsellors and those they have acquired from in-service training, both within and outside the Centre; the needs and demands of those who come seeking help; and the accumulating experience of interventions that seem to have been helpful and those that do not. The results of a follow-up study, recently conducted at the Centre, will then be reported. This will begin to show how far the theories and clinical impressions of the counsellors, and the initial aims of the project, are matched by the clients' accounts of their counselling experience and their reports of its outcome.

Chapter 2

The nature of the work

I have given a brief description of the development of the Isis Centre during its first ten years, and I would like to stress that it is still in the process of evolving and maturing. I shall try to indicate some of the principal elements of the work as it now appears, but it will be clear that there are still many questions to answer and possibilities to explore. The twin goals of responding to the needs of the community in a flexible way, and of providing a setting in which the individual counsellors may offer and develop their varied skills, both require some fluidity of model and method. Since there are, indeed, considerable differences between counsellors in individual style and in method of approach to clients and their problems, I must also emphasise that my view is a personal one. It cannot accurately represent the views of all the counsellors on all points. I shall try, however, to define some of the characteristics that are essential to the Isis Centre and its mode of work, and which hold true for most of the interactions there between counsellor and client.

I should first, perhaps, comment on the use of the term 'client' in this context. Since we are not offering a medical service, and since the people who come to the Isis Centre are not passive recipients of 'treatment' in the conventional sense, it is not appropriate to refer to them as 'patients'. In some ways the word 'customers' would be an accurate term, in as far as it implies involvement in a transaction in which the person who comes in is free to inspect or test the goods on offer, and to decide for himself whether they are, or are likely to become, what he is seeking. He exercises an active, responsible choice in the matter. This term has been adopted to some extent in the United States to describe those who approach self-referral mental health clinics (Lazare, Eisenthal and Wasserman, 1975). It seems to us that the word 'client' has some of the same implications as 'customer', but with fewer associations of a direct financial transaction. It also has acquired a particular connotation from its use by Carl Rogers and those who practise a 'client-centred' form of therapy. In that context, as in our own, it is intended to imply: 'one who comes actively and voluntarily to gain help on a problem, but without any notion of surrendering his own responsibility for the situation' (Rogers, 1951).

Self-referral

I have suggested already the significance for the Isis Centre of being distinct from a medical setting. The fact that the person who comes is not regarded as a psychiatric patient has both legal and psychological advantages. There is no formal change of status involved, and no technical threat to employment, credit or travel. There is also freedom from some of the frightening mythology of madness which, even if misplaced, is still for some people powerfully associated with the ideas of psychiatrists and psychiatric hospitals. A troubled person who would resist being referred for a consultation in a hospital setting may find it possible to walk into a self-referral centre and ask for help with his difficulties.

The concept of self-referral is fundamental to the Isis Centre. Although many people do first hear of it through their family doctors or some other professional source, it is still expected that they will make their own approach. They then choose their own time to do so and make their own arrangements. The Centre is responsible directly to the client, and has no obligation to contact anyone else about him. The basic premise is of confidentiality within the team; any step outside that has to be mutually agreed between counsellor and client. In some cases it does indeed seem to be in the client's interests for contact to be made with someone else, who knows him well, and who has, perhaps, been aware of his difficulties. If, for example, he had discussed his worries with a doctor and been prescribed some medication, it would be appropriate to let the doctor know that the client had decided to talk things over with a counsellor. Such contacts are made only with the client's permission. If a client tells his counsellor that he is already in therapy elsewhere, or that he is receiving psychiatric treatment, his permission is sought for contact to be made with the therapist or psychiatrist concerned. It would not be professionally acceptable, nor is it likely to be in his best interests, to proceed with an alternative or additional counselling contact, without due consideration. If he does not wish this contact to be made and the question discussed, further sessions at the Isis Centre cannot be offered.

I have spoken of assured confidentiality 'within the team', that is, not necessarily confined to individual counsellors. It will be clear that one of the strengths of the Isis Centre approach lies in the fact of having a group of counsellors drawn from different disciplines. They act as resources for one another, and the group as a whole has a consultative function for each member. Not all cases are discussed, either with a supervisor or in a group, but a large proportion are presented, because they involve particular difficulties or are of especial interest in some way. Just as a client is free to use his counsellor as a resource, to assist him in thinking about his problems, so each counsellor is held to be entitled to consult with other members of the team. In each case, the initiative lies with the individual client or counsellor: opportunities for sharing and learning are open to him, if he takes them up. In each case, also, the act of sharing experiences with another or others, and endeavouring to think aloud about them, makes possible the emergence of less conscious aspects of those experiences, and new ways of approaching them. The counsellor's own involvement in a process of voluntary consultation increases his empathy with his clients, to whom he himself offers just such an opportunity.

It should be emphasised that the decision to approach any resource for the purpose of discussing one's intimate problems frankly with another person is by no means an easy one. It requires a high degree of motivation, either consciously thought out or as a product of intense distress. Many clients have described the difficulty of coming through the door on the first occasion. To succeed in doing so involves often an appreciable amount of courage and commitment. This very fact, however, lays the foundation for a serious relationship which can lead to useful change. To insist on the principle of self-referral is to allow a self-selection process to operate. The results of this process are then respected, even if people come who might otherwise have been regarded rather doubtfully as candidates for useful counselling or psychotherapy. Unless some obvious misunderstanding has occurred as to the nature of the Centre's work, it may well be that the troubled person is himself the best judge of what may help him. The limits of the work that can then take place are determined by: the experience and skills of the counsellor; the capacity of the client for thinking psychologically and for managing his anxiety; and the resources of the Centre, which is not in a position to offer either psychoanalysis or very long-term support. Great care is taken to respond to the client at the level at which he is seeking and can tolerate intervention, so that the limits of his capacity to bear anxiety are not over-stepped.

The process of self-referral has two other aspects that are important: the client himself defines the problem that troubles him, rather than relying on someone else's expert diagnosis; and he also chooses the time at which he takes steps to find some help. A very wide range of problems is presented at the Centre, and care is taken to hear how a person describes his difficulties. This may tell a good deal about his view of the world and his characteristic pattern of adaptation. Attention is also paid to his reasons for coming at a particular moment. The special nature of the current stress, that has been decisive in convincing him that he cannot manage alone any longer, is important for an understanding both of his strengths and his particular vulnerabilities. Furthermore, the moment that the client chooses to come is likely to be the one when he is particularly open to change. Caplan (1964) makes a case for providing resources for people when they feel themselves to be in crisis, either internally or in their external circumstances. They are at such times highly motivated to make constructive changes, and to do so may have a long-term preventive effect, in that they are not thrown back on ill-judged, maladaptive devices for surviving the difficult period.

The first meeting

It may be helpful, in order to convey something of the nature of the work that takes place in this setting, to describe some of the counsellor's concerns on the first occasion of meeting with a stranger who may choose to become a 'client'. On going to the waiting-room to collect him or her, he will know little more than a name, and perhaps whether this person originally telephoned or called in to make the appointment.

As at any meeting of strangers, each is alert to the signals conveyed by the appearance and manner of the other. The counsellor is interested in the way this person chooses to dress and present himself, and in his bearing as he enters this new situation. Information of a non-verbal kind is conveyed throughout the first meeting. This not only concerns the new person's basic style, but also his experience here and now, particularly as expressed by fine *changes* of manner in the course of the session. Much depends on this initial meeting, and on the changes in levels of anxiety or trust, hope or misgiving that are occasioned by it.

The client will be invited to explain what brings him to the Centre. Some people will embark on this straightaway; others need a space for some preliminary questioning and orientation. The counsellor observes, and possibly reflects aloud upon, the degree of difficulty experienced by the client in sharing his troubled feelings with another person. He is interested to gather what the client hopes, expects or fears to be likely outcomes of this situation, and maybe to discover the route he has taken to enter it.

As the new client begins to explain the difficulties in which he finds himself, a certain pattern of emphases begins to appear. He will tend to describe the sources of his distress as rather more outside himself or rather more within; as mainly located in his circumstances and in others to whom he relates, or as chiefly arising in his own private world of feelings and fantasies. He may complain of kinds of behaviour which he, or others, find worrying or unacceptable, or he may describe physical symptoms that embody his distress. A time dimension also starts to come clear, suggesting the relation of the present problems to events in the past or to feared aspects of the future. As he speaks he will begin to convey the relative proportions of anxiety, grief, anger, fear, disappointment and other affects associated with his problems, and also whether he tends to view these experiences with alarm, with despair, or with a measure of self-observant interest. The counsellor begins to discover whether this person has, or can develop or recover, some degree of curiosity about his emotional experiences, which may lead itself to some shared work towards understanding them.

In asking about, or simply listening for, the reasons for the client's choosing this particular time for coming for help, the counsellor may be wondering why a hitherto relatively effective system of defences has recently been threatened or breached; or why a clearly precarious balance has been newly upset, maybe as it has many times before. He is interested to hear of disturbing recent events, not only in terms of their direct impact but also of the imagery they may carry. For example, a relatively trivial parting or disappointment, or a minor argument or disagreement, may have started up echoes of earlier experiences of more serious loss or conflict, that have not been adequately grieved or resolved. By means of a simple question, perhaps as to whether the client has ever felt like this before, the counsellor begins the process of linking the present to the past. This helps to clarify whether there are particular kinds of stress that repeatedly prove hard to bear, as for example, confrontation, loss, or change. It may also shed light on the customary recovery systems that have hitherto been employed. These may include, as now, the impulse to seek appropriate help, or may seem to be characteristically based on less constructive mechanisms, such as denial, or flight, or projection of the unwanted feelings.

As the client speaks, with some questioning help from the counsellor as seems necessary, the current context of his life begins to come clear. This includes matters such as where and with whom he lives, what he does, and the kinds of satisfactions and difficulties associated for him with other people, and with his daily activities. Spontaneously or invited, he may also describe something of his family background, and the quality of relationships within it.

I stress that the counsellor is primarily 'listening for' rather than 'asking about' these areas of information, as he gradually builds up a picture and a sense of the person who is with him. It is important that the emphasis is determined by the client, and some kinds of information seem significant simply because they have been omitted. The counsellor is especially likely to be alerted to any aspect of experience which is mentioned very fleetingly, yet leaves in his, the listener's, mind a feeling of special attentiveness, interest or even pain, which seems disproportionate to the minimal emphasis it has received in the client's presentation. He may later want to draw attention back to such an area, or merely bear it in mind, for future clarification. The prior task is to relate to the world in which the client lives, as *he* presently perceives it.

Meanwhile the client is orientating himself in this new situation, with this unknown person. He has been offered a certain amount of quiet space and time, and a person who listens seriously. He may be surprised by elements of his own response, as he finds this experience threatening, bewildering, reassuring, exciting, relieving or disappointing, in various degrees. The counsellor will sufficiently resemble or sharply contrast with a preconceived expectation that the client may or may not have known he brought with him. Some reflection on these experiences, with the counsellor helping him to think aloud about them, paves the way towards a decision as to whether or not he will want to return. Some clients will feel, towards the end of the first session, which lasts for fifty minutes, that they have only just begun to explain a long and complicated story; others, having succinctly summarised the trouble in the first few minutes, will already feel they have been there a long time, perhaps too long. Some will feel that their pre-existing fear that no one will ever understand has been confirmed; others may be appalled at the surprising and distressing things that have already poured out, and have very mixed feelings about this; others again may feel some hope awakened through an experience of being received and heard. Out of some joint consideration of such feelings arises a plan to meet or not to meet again, or, in many cases, an agreement to meet a few more times, for further exploration of the problem and of the question of whether a counselling approach feels likely to be helpful. At an agreed time the matter is again reviewed, when a decision to stop may be taken, or a plan may be made to continue for a specific number of sessions, or in an open-ended way, as seems appropriate to that particular relationship.

On-going work

One way of thinking about the nature of the work is to consider the basic paradox on which it rests: that is, that the counsellor offers the client an opportunity for security and attachment, in the full expectation that this experience will lead to increased autonomy. The goal is greater freedom of independent movement and thought for the client, but it is recognised that a means to this end is the experience of a reliable relationship, in which the client may recognise and grow more tolerant of the dependent as well as the independent aspects of his personality. The work of John Bowlby is of special relevance, in that he stresses that self-reliance grows from opportunities to rely on others and not be let down, and that freedom and autonomy are integrally linked with capacities for, and experiences based on, trust and attachment (Bowlby, 1979). He describes the therapeutic situation as providing for the client 'a secure base from which to explore'. The explorations may be imagined both in terms of the client's daring to think and experience his real thoughts and feelings, and in terms of his understanding and developing relationships, both with the therapist and in the outside world.

These dual strands, the provision of security and the expectation of increased self-reliance, are embodied in the structure of the work at the Isis Centre. If a client agrees to work with a counsellor over a period of time, he is offered a regular appointment at the same time each week. These fifty minutes each week belong to him and although the time cannot be extended, it will not be either shortened or interrupted. He will see the same person in the same room, and the time is his. These very provisions have a double nature. Although safety, reliability and confidentiality may form the foundations for trust, the offer of an intimate, on-going relationship may be daunting as well as comforting. Since it is in the area of making and sustaining relationships that many clients find difficulty, anxieties are bound to arise in the counselling situation too. The object is to create a climate in which these anxieties can be experienced, expressed and resolved, as opposed to denied or evaded.

Similarly, fifty minutes is both a long and a very short time. Anthony Storr (1979), in his discussion of the therapeutic relationship, stresses the ways in which it contrasts with ordinary social exchanges. Very rarely does one person offer another his relaxed and undivided attention, freed from both external distractions and from the natural impulses to share or compete that arise in normal conversation. This offers the client an opportunity for an unusual degree of continuity of introspective thought and experience. This, however, is also a challenge, for it implies the expectation that he will *use* the time, and enter into an active and co-operative effort with his counsellor in trying to understand what is happening in his life.

I have said that the sessions, while in some perspectives lengthy, may also seem very short and restricted. This is certainly so, whether one considers a single session in relation to the client's experiences in the whole of a week, or a series of sessions in relation to his total life. Embarking on a close relationship under such circumstances involves not only support and sustenance but also an awareness of endings and loss. There is a strong expectation in our work that clients will be enabled to experience the feelings that arise, but also to tolerate the necessary boundaries of the sessions and to contain their anxiety from week to week. It is our experience that the achievement of this degree of containment, accompanied by a reliable provision of attention and shared work, helps a person both to recognise his feelings and to take responsibility for what he does as a result of them.

The role of the counsellor

I have mentioned two main types of goals for our work: understanding and increased self-reliance. The ways to both lie through the experience of the relationship with the counsellor, and through the thinking work that can take place within that relationship. The aim then is the generalisation of the new learning to relationships and activities outside the sessions.

In speaking of increased autonomy I mean to suggest greater freedom and self-direction, both internal and external. Much confused unhappiness is the result of conflicting motives and feelings; these become buried beneath successive strata of only partially effective systems for denying or evading the mental pain they cause. If this muddle can be patiently disentangled and the original conflict exposed, it can be re-experienced, re-evaluated and, perhaps, resolved in a more direct way. Accomplishing even some steps towards this result leads to a person feeling less driven by his internal conflicts. He becomes more able to exercise choice of response and to adapt to internal and external realities in a more constructive way. This experience of greater inner freedom allows for increased expressiveness and fulfilment in current relationships and activities.

Such freedoms depend to a large extent on understanding, and the counselling process seeks to make more of experience intelligible. The counsellor maintains the expectation that events in a person's mental life can be understood, and he offers a model of exploration. He considers with the client his current conflicts and distress, and tries to understand how these relate to other aspects of his present life, and how they relate to his past. The client is in possession of a daunting quantity of information about his own life, composed not only of facts, but also of feelings, memories, and secret wishes and fears. He may be confused by the mass of detail, and afraid or ashamed of various aspects, some of which he excludes from his awareness. The counsellor, encumbered with less detail, may be able to see patterns and kinds of continuity which help the client to experience his life in a meaningful way. He may also be able to help him contemplate those aspects that had hitherto seemed unbearably frightening or shameful. Seeing more clearly the links between the past and the present, the client is in a stronger position for making realistic plans for the future. He will know his own capacities more accurately and be less confused by fantastic hopes and fears.

In the sessions the client is free to bring whatever material is on his mind. The counsellor typically takes the role of listening, responding, or asking questions to clarify what is being said. He may contribute ideas, associations or interpretations, but he essentially tries to stay with or follow the client, rather than leading him. His special contribution is to clarify and draw attention to linking themes as they emerge, and to be alert to the client's patterns of relating and responding. These are revealed in the material the client brings and in the developing counselling relationship. Just as one goal of the work for the client may be said to be greater integration of thinking and feeling, so the counsellor tries to be alert to and to make use of both his intellectual and his emotional responses to the client.

Kinds of change that may be expected

A successful intervention might be thought of as one in which the relationship becomes sufficiently established that the client feels safe to admit into awareness some at least of his conflicting feelings. He is then enabled to think afresh about the troubling areas in his experience, and to become free to tackle them in new ways.

The counsellor consistently models both accuracy and tolerance. The client is encouraged to think more honestly about his motives and feelings, but in an atmosphere of acceptance. He has a greater possibility of making responsible choices if he dares to know about his weaknesses and destructive impulses, than if he wishes them away or denies them. First it is necessary to acknowledge them without experiencing excessive shame or guilt, and this can be accomplished in the company of another person who is seen to be able to bear them.

The client is clearly embarking on work which will at times be painful and disconcerting. Attitudes to himself and others that he has previously made the foundation of his behaviour and relationships cannot be relinquished without some anxiety. Change, even towards a more hopeful or constructive position, involves movement into unfamiliar territory, and this is inevitably alarming (Wolff, 1977). Nevertheless, even in striving to accomplish such changes, the client may be expected gradually to experience greater self-confidence and self-esteem. These derive both from the felt regard of the counsellor, and from the real achievement of the difficult work he is himself doing.

Fears of madness or illness may be dispelled as the work proceeds. These fears are often rooted in the panic of having apparently incomprehensible feelings and impulses. The more fearful he becomes, the more a person turns his intelligence away from contemplating his terrors. When he is helped to turn his thoughts around and use them constructively, fears are reduced as his experience becomes intelligible.

Another change that may be expected is improvement in the client's personal relationships. As the trust that he places in his relationship with his counsellor is not betrayed, he is likely to become more hopeful about and trusting of relationships in general. As he becomes more open and more expressive towards other people, so he begins to elicit warmer responses from them. His increased powers of observation and reflection also allow him to pause before reacting impulsively, and to choose from a wider range of possible initiatives and responses. Storr (1960) has observed that the development and maturity of the individual, and the maturity of his relationships with others, are inseparably linked. If a climate is created in which a person can advance towards the realisation of his own capacities and a confident acceptance of himself, so he will be able to relate to others in a more direct and satisfying way.

One familiar outcome, that is emphasised by Malan (1979), also concerns the way in which a person relates to others. This involves movement in the client from an attitude of either excessive passivity or excessive aggression, to what Malan has described as 'constructive self-assertion'. He sees this as an element in the improvement of almost every successful case. Our clients do indeed speak of having become either 'less of a door-mat' or less likely to come to blows with people. This involves taking up responsibility for and entitlement to an appropriate degree of assertiveness. This process may be facilitated by its exploration within and outside the counselling relationship.

I have outlined here some of the processes involved in the course of a counselling interaction, and some of the goals towards which these are directed. I have suggested some kinds of change that may be expected to take place for the client. These ideas are based both on theory, and on an accumulation of clinical impressions and clients' spontaneous reports, gathered over the ten years of the Isis Centre's life. The main object of this book is to compare these thoughts with the reported experiences of a group of clients who agreed to tell us, in a systematic way, what their hopes and experiences had been. We wished to test the accuracy of our impressions by their accounts. I shall first describe how the follow-up study, by means of which we gathered this information, was designed and executed.

Chapter 3

Background of the study

In the first chapter, I indicated some of the considerations that led to the opening of the Isis Centre. I have also sketched its history, and outlined the basic principles of the therapeutic work that is undertaken there. A further aspect of the work has involved efforts to study it systematically, in order to be able to describe it accurately, and to evaluate its effectiveness, and also to provide a model that may be of interest to others.

Why research?

It seemed important for several reasons to study the work as it evolved. The primary one was that the Isis Centre was established as a pilot project within the National Health Service. It therefore carried the responsibility of trying to judge its effectiveness and relevance as far as local needs were concerned, and also of predicting whether its style of working might be applicable more generally. Now, some ten years later, it has a fairly clear, if still evolving identity, and it seems appropriate to share some of the experience that has been accumulated, and to draw some conclusions as to the usefulness of this style of service.

A second reason for studying the work is intrinsic to the counselling process itself. It is essential that the counsellor tries to be as aware as possible of what is happening between himself and his client. This fundamentally rests on his sensitivity and perceptiveness in each particular interaction, and these qualities are supported and enhanced within the existing framework of supervision and case discussions. Another dimension is added, however, if experiences can be pooled and compared in an intelligible way, so that the constant factors emerge, as well as the unique details.

Research in this setting, therefore, has both internal and external purposes. The former concern increasing our own understanding of what we are doing, and attempting to do it more effectively; the latter concern the representation of this work to others, as a contribution to the growing range of mental health services.

Methods adopted so far

At first we simply began to gather together what we knew about the people who came to the Centre. Some background facts had been routinely recorded by counsellors, and a little more attention was paid to this, not in efforts to find out more than that which naturally arose in the course of the counselling contact, but in order not to lose what was known.

In 1975, a careful study of a hundred consecutive clients was undertaken, to look at such factors as age, sex and marital status; the problems that people presented; their reasons for coming at a particular time; their reasons for choosing the Isis Centre; and the number of times each person came (Agulnik, Holroyd and Mandelbrote, 1976). Since then such information has been gathered for all the clients each year.

Data of this kind allow us to compose a general sketch of Isis Centre clients as a whole. Between two and three hundred new people are seen each year. About a third of them come only once; nearly half come for from two to ten weekly sessions; and the remainder have a longer contact with the Centre, sometimes extending to a year or more. Total attendances number around 2,500 each year.

Clients are rather more likely to be women than men, in the ratio of about three to two. The women are more likely than the men to be, or to have been, married, and to have children. About a third of all clients have already had some contact with formal psychiatric services, either for consultation or for treatment. The most frequently presented problems consistently include: distressing feelings, especially of depression or anxiety; problems in relationships, both particular and general; and difficulties in working, studying and coping with everyday tasks.

Some other kinds of investigation have been undertaken in relation to the work of the Centre. One of these involved contacting and sharing experiences with other agencies doing related work, in Oxford, and in other parts of the country. This helped to establish a perspective within which to view the work undertaken in this setting. The other was to establish on-going workshops, in which counsellors could share and study their work as it unfolded, with the particular aims of clarifying process, goals, and kinds of outcome. The third kind of research, a follow-up study, provided the material which forms the basis of the remainder of this book.

The follow-up study; early considerations

It will be clear that what was missing so far in terms of information about the work was any direct comment, systematically gathered, from the clients themselves about their experiences. As counsellors we had recorded some facts, thoughts and impressions, and sometimes some tentative predictions as to outcome. We were building up a shared ethos, and some individual variations on it, on the basis of theory and of clinical impressions. Was it possible to test this, to see how far it corresponded with clients' feelings and experiences?

Among research studies designed to consider the process and outcome of counselling and therapy of various kinds, there are remarkably few instances of researchers directly asking the consumer about his experience. Therapists of the analytic school have tended to consider that patients' reports would be too partial and distorted to be very valuable, and those working within behavioural systems have been impatient for quantifiable findings. Research effort has, therefore, been heavily weighted towards factors which may be clear to study, but which may also be of doubtful relevance, since they are almost exclusively drawn from the preconceptions of the researcher, rather than from the experience of the client. The undirected responses of people to open-ended questions about their experience promise to give rich but possibly unmanageable material. Nevertheless, it is likely that here lie the most fruitful starting points for understanding the complex process of therapy. Feifel and Eels (1963), observing the scarcity of information about the client's experience of therapy, wrote: 'Our view is, despite the stumbling blocks marring this way of advance, that the involved parties in psychotherapy are still in the most favored position to provide us with promising leads concerning what takes place.'

Strupp and his colleagues (1969) also took this view when they conducted their study of the patients' view of psychotherapy, as did Mayer and Timms (1970), when they collected accounts of their experience from people who had sought help from the Family Welfare Association. Mayer and Timms consider the reasons for the relative neglect of the client's viewpoint, and argue for it as a source of understanding of helping relationships, and also of directions for future research. More recently, Llewelyn and Hume (1979) took this position as a basis for their study of the factors that people consistently found most helpful, in contrasting kinds of therapy.

There is clearly a growing interest in the client's view of therapy as a legitimate focus of study, and as a valuable source of insight into the process. Nevertheless, several important issues still gave us pause. One was a fear of intruding on clients, in disregard for the principles of respect and confidentiality that are the foundations of the work. Another was concern that heightened self-consciousness on the part of the counsellors involved in such a study might interfere with the delicate and complicated relationships between them and their clients. It was imperative that any study undertaken should aim to reflect the

23

work without intruding on it or altering it. Care had particularly to be taken that the fact of having participated in the research should interfere as little as possible with a client's freedom to make contact with his counsellor again at a later date, should he wish this.

We also had to consider the time and manpower that were available. The study was to be financed by a grant from the Regional Health Authority, which would support the work of one researcher for a day and a half per week for a year. This was later extended at the rate of one day per week for a further three years. This was to be the basic investment of time, supplemented by the co-operation and contributions of all the counsellors who took part in the study. The author, who was the principal researcher, is also one of the counsellors at the Centre: it was felt that the problems this might present as far as objectivity is concerned were outweighed by the need for the researcher to be thoroughly conversant with the work of the Centre, and with the psychodynamic principles on which it is based.

The method chosen

We were interested in the reasons for a person's approaching the Centre and his experiences there, as well as in the outcome of the counselling contact. We had, therefore, to evolve a way of producing accounts of what had happened in each case, that would be as accurate as possible without being intrusive.

To this end, we developed two parallel questionnaires, one to be completed by the counsellor and one by the client. The aim of the questions was to build up a picture of the contact through all its stages. We were concerned with the decisions made at the beginning: for example, the reasons for a person's coming; his choice of a particular time for seeking help; his selection of the Isis Centre; and his hopes and expectations on coming in. Then we wanted to observe the various decisions made in the course of the counselling; such as, those concerning the number of sessions, the agreed task and the nature of the work. Finally, we wanted to understand how termination was reached, and what kind of outcome was achieved. (A copy of the questionnaire used will be found in Appendix II.)

The counsellor in each case completed his account in the form of a written questionnaire, soon after the client terminated his sessions. Clients were invited to come for an interview, based on the same questions, or, if that were inconvenient or impossible, to complete a questionnaire. This request was made about a month after they had ceased to attend the Centre, and they were asked to provide their information in six months' time, so that we could see whether any effects attributed to the counselling were lasting. This also gave time for the immediate feelings about termination to have been worked through. (The letter that was sent to each client in the study is included in Appendix I.)

Our final decision concerned who was to be included in the study sample. As I have mentioned, about a third of our clients come only once to the Centre; about half have a fairly brief series of sessions; and the remainder come over a longer period of time. It seemed to be impracticable and possibly unreasonable to ask for accounts from the very short-term clients, for many of whom we might not even have a means of contact. Nevertheless, we were interested to understand some of the factors which might distinguish them as a group from those who came longer. Consequently, counsellors completed forms for *all* clients who came during the study period, while we sought follow-up information only from those clients who had come four or more times. Thus we did have some points of comparison available across the whole sample, although not always in terms of client feed-back.

We took for the study a period of four consecutive months. All people who were seen during that period, whether they had already been coming for some time or whether they arrived as new clients, were included in the sample.

The pilot study

When we had developed the questions to be used in the study, and had agreed that we, as counsellors, would attempt to answer them, we still had to ascertain whether it would be possible to collect clients' accounts too. To this end, we conducted a small pilot study. Seventeen people were contacted, all of whom had terminated their attendance at the Centre more than six months before. They were chosen to represent as wide a range of contacts with the Isis Centre as possible. Of these seventeen, thirteen clients responded and expressed willingness to participate in the study. Of these, three had come for fewer than ten counselling sessions; six had come between ten and twenty times; and four had come longer, up to sixty times. Five men of the six we contacted agreed to participate, as did eight women of the eleven we wrote to. Nine people came for interview at the Centre; three completed questionnaires; and one was interviewed at home.

This pilot study did, then, establish that clients would agree to participate in the study. Several expressed some satisfaction in being able to let us know how things had turned out for them. Some clients feel free to do this anyway, while others, it seems, feel uncertain as to whether this is appropriate. Others said that they were glad of an opportunity to reflect aloud on their experience. Our anxieties about intruding on people were somewhat allayed by these responses, as also by the freedom taken by some clients not to participate.

The questions involved in the interview or questionnaire did also

25

seem to be relevant to clients' experiences, and the informal atmosphere established in the interview made it possible for clients to add comments in addition to those involved in answering the standard questions. All information of this kind was noted down. In no case, in the pilot or the follow-up study itself, was the client interviewed by his original counsellor. This was to allow freedom of response, not limited by the constraints of the counselling relationship. Where clients of the researcher-counsellor were involved, a colleague conducted the interviews. Preparatory discussion of method, and experience gained in the pilot study, ensured that the style of the two interviewers was as consistent as possible.

One other purpose of the pilot study was, of course, to see whether the question forms would discriminate between different kinds of experience, and whether they would reveal a range of outcome. That they *were* illuminating in these ways may be illustrated by a brief look at the outcome of the pilot study.

Some early findings

The clients who agreed to participate in the pilot study described a variety of ways of using the opportunity offered at the Centre, and here they are grouped to illustrate some kinds of outcome, as they experienced it. They are presented in order of degree of apparent change.

Firstly, there were two women, one of twenty-four, the other in her early thirties, who said they had experienced no change at all. One had come for nineteen sessions and the other for six. The latter said that it was 'not what I wanted'; she was 'relieved when it was over'. She had hoped for specific advice as to how to solve her problems of loneliness and depression; she had felt very impatient of anything other than practical directions. The person who came nineteen times expressed much more ambivalence about the experience: she came eagerly into the room for the follow-up interview, saying how important this work is, and then proceeded to deny that it had had any effect for her at all. She insisted, 'I'd have got through the same period in the same sort of way and time anyway.' She remembered material and interpretations from the sessions very vividly, but indignantly denied their relevance. It was hard to assess the value of the experience for her, or to explain the fact that she had persisted with it so long. One clear characteristic, however, of both these interactions was that no warm bond seemed to have been established with the counsellor.

'Left me a bit cold, the whole business.'
'Didn't feel terrific sympathy with my counsellor.'
'I got the feeling that I was wasting her time.'

These then are two examples at one end of the spectrum, where it seems the relationship failed to be established and the other aspects of the work could not really be used.

Another woman, who was thirty-three, was emphatic that the changes she accomplished were very limited. She came in to join her husband in marital work, and was insistent from the start that her interest was primarily to help him rather than herself. She did acknowledge some improvement in their relationship but attributed that mainly to changes in her husband.

Then there was a group of three men, who came respectively fifteen, fourteen and twenty-six times. One was twenty-five years old; the others thirty-three and thirty-eight. Each of them suffered from long-standing anxiety and depression, deep-seated attitudes of pessimism and despair, and very low self-esteem. They each came in at a time of acute crisis, feeling suicidal, utterly despairing. Each at follow-up said that he felt he had been retrieved from complete break-down or suicide, but they seemed to have been restored to a state only slightly less anxious than before. In each of these three cases the relationship with the counsellor, its warmth and security, seems to have been of great importance, but little use had been made of the opportunity for insight, or reflecting on their experiences. They had adopted slightly different modes of warding off their anxiety and depression: more resignation, some bitterness, some relying on the idea of the Isis Centre's continuing existence for comfort and reassurance. Each reported less fear of complete break-down in the future. It felt as though the counselling relationship had shored them up against their anxiety; their problems seemed less overwhelming, but no more comprehensible than before.

The remaining seven people, that is slightly more than half, described effects which seemed to stem both from that part of the experience which derives from a warm, secure relationship, based on mutual respect, and from that part which offers and expects quite strenuous rethinking and exploring of experience.

Two young women (twenty-four years and twenty-two years), who came respectively only nine and six times, illustrate an important part of our work. Of a sample of 100 consecutive clients that we had studied previously, 52 were in their late teens or twenties. For many of these clients, the central problem concerns the difficulties involved in separating from the parental home, and establishing an independent life, without experiencing overwhelming fear, guilt, resentment or conflict. Each of these young women in the pilot study had been blocked and immobilised by aspects of her relationship with her parents, which were preventing her from getting on with her own specific tasks. In one case this was her marriage: anger and pain associated with her father's death, and its consequences for her life, were feeding jealousy and resentment of her husband and child, and preventing her from developing her own personality and her roles as wife and mother. In the other case an intelligent, creative girl was finding herself unable to study. She had a history of bouts of severe depression and a variety of physical symptoms; she had had some psychiatric consultations and medication. She was now hesitating to complete her academic course, because, it emerged, she could not see how to reconcile her own plans for the future with her parents' hopes and wishes; she dreaded the confrontation, certain she would be swayed from her own course and very resentful about this, in anticipation. Each did limited, focused work on her problems, putting her current difficulties in the perspective of her whole life, understanding better her real feelings and motives, and experiencing a release and new confidence. For example, the girl who had been relying on anti-depressants for some time found she no longer needed them. She said, 'The change was from being a person who needed drugs to being confident and able to cope. But, most important, I feel I will be able to cope better with any similar episode in the future.' This was the girl who came only six times, and who was reporting changes more than six months later. She had completed her degree and had been accepted for the further professional training of her choice. Relations with her parents were warmer and much less strained, although she had insisted on following her own choice of career. (She called in, of her own accord, eighteen months later, to let her counsellor know that her plans were working out well and she had had no recurrence of her depression.)

There were a further five people, for whom the greatest degree of change seems to have taken place. They described complex interactions, which ranged in duration from twelve to sixty sessions. All of these people spoke of having done some profound rethinking of characteristic ways of viewing themselves, relating to others, and interpreting experience. In every case there had been a close and involved relationship with the counsellor, mobilising and clarifying intense feelings, both positive and negative. Several people mentioned an early 'nursery disappointment' that their counsellors did not offer reassurance and advice, but they went on from there to take the initiative themselves and to be surprised and pleased to find what they were capable of.

They spoke of being able to be both more accurate about and more accepting of themselves:

'I know who I am; I know what I am.'
'I had originally wanted to be made into someone else; now I accept myself more.'
'I stopped being afraid of myself and my feelings.'
'I feel much more at home, at ease with myself.'

This last man speaks of still having some

'fear and anxiety about others, yet now I can cope with it by recognising it as real and understanding it, and not hating myself for it.'

Several of these people had hitherto been tossing between extremes of feeling guilty and of feeling persecuted. They spoke of now being able to consider events without so rapidly apportioning blame. This was accompanied by an increased capacity to pause, observe, and reflect on experience — to ask, 'Why?' Needless to say, it is not always possible to answer this question completely, but even where people had become more acutely aware of the 'contradictions' involved in living, they had also become more tolerant of them. Perhaps they became interested rather than frightened by them.

The internal changes they experienced and reported were also said to have positive effects in their lives outside the sessions, in relationships, work, and physical well-being. People spoke of improved relationships with members of their families; for example, the young woman who had been so resentful of her first child, who had been accidentally conceived, consciously chose to have another baby, and said she was now enjoying her family, while also making constructive plans for her life as a whole. A man who came in in anguish lest he harm his son in violent rages, reported that he no longer comes to blows with people; he has much more confidence that he can express himself in words, and indeed by talking rather than shouting. A woman of forty-four who had been entangled in a bitter relationship with her mother was able to move away and establish an independent home for herself, while also being able to relate to her mother in a warmer and more tolerant way. One man also said,

'During the course of my counselling I seem to have decided I didn't need to be ill any more. So I gave up drugs, haven't needed to see a doctor, and feel very well. I also feel more at home in, and happy with, my body.'

Our position, therefore, on completion of the pilot study, was that it was likely that we would have a satisfactory response rate from clients for our follow-up study, and that the forms we had devised would discriminate between different kinds of experience. More than half of the clients in the pilot study had reported significant changes, in feelings, relationships and personal effectiveness, and had indicated some of the factors in the counselling with which these changes were associated. It remained, then, to see whether these cases proved representative of Isis Centre clients as a whole; to look in detail at the interactions involved; and to look at the characteristics of those who settle to work with a counsellor at the Centre, in comparison with those of people who come briefly and leave.

Chapter 4

The follow-up study: clients' problems

Work was then begun on the follow-up study itself. The sample consisted of the 144 people who came for counselling during a period of four months. As planned, counsellors completed their form of the questionnaire as these clients finished their sessions at the Centre, whether they had come only once or over an extended period of time.

We had decided that clients who came to the Isis Centre fewer than four times would not be contacted. There were also some instances in which the counsellor concerned advised against follow-up contact being made with a person who had come for more than four sessions, and this advice was respected. If the interests of a client seemed to be at odds with those of the research, they were given priority. This occurred sometimes in cases where termination had been difficult to achieve, or still felt uncertain. There were also some instances of a client moving on to a therapist in another setting, where it was felt that the new relationship might not yet be securely established. In such situations it felt unwise to initiate another kind of contact from the Centre. All such cases were reviewed six months after termination, and, if the original doubt about making contact no longer seemed to have foundation, the client was then approached.

In cases where the request for follow-up information was made normally but the client did not reply, at either the first contact or at the second one, further efforts were made, six months later, to reach him, and these were sometimes successful. The final numbers involved in the study may be seen in Table 4.1.

We have, therefore, material of various kinds on which to draw, in order to try to understand the experience of those people who came to the Isis Centre during the period of the study. We have accounts from the counsellors of their contacts with all the clients they saw during this time; and we have detailed accounts of their experience from 52 clients, that is, 71 per cent of those we approached. These descriptions are

TABLE 4.1. The follow-up study

	Total	Men	Women
Total number of sample	144	53	91
Total contacted for follow-up	73	25	48
followed up	52	18	34
no reply	11	4	7
declined to participate	4	1	3
agreed but failed to attend			
interview or complete questionnaire	6	2	4
Continuing	5	2	3
Excluded from follow-up			
those who came only once	31	12	19
those who came 2−3 times	16	9	7
counsellor advised against follow-up	15	4	11
no address available	4	1	3

retrospective, at a distance of at least six months, and show both the benefits and the disadvantages of this fact. Some of the immediate feelings at termination had been dealt with, so that the experience could be reviewed as a whole, and its salient features described. People sometimes found it hard to remember specific details of arrangements or agreements, but no one had difficulty in naming some features that had seemed important to him. Because the questionnaire was compiled in such a way as to reconstruct the steps taken into, through and out of counselling, people seemed to be able to re-enter the experience and recall it vividly. In the interview they were encouraged to talk freely, material being noted down in the relevant sections as it was recalled, and specific questions later being asked and filled in if they had not already been covered. The result is a rich collection of spontaneous comments, vividly remembered moments and thoughtful recollections, as well as systematic data on specific points. ·

I shall first present this material with the aim of giving an overall picture of the troubles, expectations and experiences of people who come to the Isis Centre. Using the 52 reports collected from clients, I shall present the reasons they gave for coming at all, and their reasons for coming at a particular time. Then we shall consider what they said of their hopes as to what they might achieve, and their expectations as to what kind of help might be provided. In the following chapters, I shall present their descriptions of what happened in their sessions at the Isis Centre, and their reports of the outcome of this experience. Throughout I shall give verbatim clients' answers to the questions, and quotations of any length will be followed by a reference number, and by the sex and age of the person speaking. (e.g. 4-M-23: client number four, a man of twenty-three years of age). The reference number provides a means of linking a quotation to the relevant case-outline. These outlines are collected in tables in chapters 9, 10, 11 and 12.

Clients' problems

A primary assumption on which the design of a counselling resource such as the Isis Centre is based, is that many people experience severe emotional distress, which they do not conceive of as medical in nature. To test this belief by the responses of people who had chosen to come for counselling, the first two questions in the interview or questionnaire concerned the nature of the problems which moved them to do so. The questions were phrased like this:

'What was the main problem troubling you when you first came to the Isis Centre?'
'Were there any other things that troubled you at that time, or that emerged in the course of the sessions?'

In answer to the second question, people tended to amplify what they had already said, and provide further detail or emphasis, so I have combined the material from both questions, to give an overall picture of the kinds of distress they were experiencing.

The most striking feature of the answers is the stress placed on the *feelings* that people were experiencing at the time of approaching the Centre. They were invited to name problems, and indeed usually specified some situation or circumstance that was particularly troubling at the time. Nevertheless, the aspect of the problem which led them to seek help was often said to be the intensity of the feeling it aroused, rather than, for example, the intrinsic difficulty of the dilemma, or the degree of external stress involved.

The most frequently presented problem, then, was experience of distress that could no longer be borne alone. The next largest group of problems concerned difficulties in relationships with other people. Sometimes these were relationships generally, 'getting on with people'; sometimes they were specific ones, with their parents, for example, or in marital or other sexual relationships, or in relating to their children. Another group of problems concerned difficulties at work or in studying, or in coping with the demands of everyday tasks generally.

Before looking in more detail at the specific problems presented, it is interesting to consider two related questions. The first of these was designed to provide a rough guide to the degree of distress the client felt he was experiencing at that time. It was phrased like this:

'Would you say that your problems then caused you: extreme, moderate or mild distress?'

This was taken as a starting point for the answer, and any additional comments were noted too.

Of the 52 people, only one person spoke of mild distress, and she was emphatic that she had come in to inquire how to relieve someone else's problems. Three other people spoke of distress being mild usually, but occasionally extreme. Twelve people rated their distress as moderate, one of them describing his efforts to conceal and control his unhappiness. Four others spoke of moderate distress, 'extreme at times'. The remaining thirty-two people had no hesitation in describing their distress as extreme, sometimes adding comments such as: 'becoming unbearable, I felt'; 'I was terribly strung-up and tearful'; 'I didn't know which way to turn'; 'I was completely at sea: I didn't see much point in anything'; 'I just thought everything was black and impossible'.

Clients were also asked to what degree they felt their problems then were interfering with everyday activities and relationships. They were again offered a rough scale: a great deal, moderately, little.

Of 52 people, six said their problems interfered little with their activities and relationships. Several of these emphasised the private nature of their troubles, and the fact that outside activities sometimes offered an escape and relief. Two women observed that their difficulties interfered a great deal at home, with their families, but little elsewhere. Eleven people spoke of moderate interference, and some of these commented that they had devised ways of dealing with their distress so that their work, for example, should not be threatened. The remaining thirty-three people said that their problems interfered with their relationships and daily activities a great deal, one adding that the disruption was 'absolutely total'.

From the answers to these two questions it can be seen that a very high level of distress was reported by many clients, often interfering badly with their daily lives. To turn back, now, to the specific problems they described, we shall look first at the feelings they named.

Distressing feelings

The feeling specified most frequently was depression. Thirteen women and five men said this was among their main problems when they first came to the Isis Centre, some adding details such as, 'I sat down and cried for hours on end', or, 'I felt so bad I almost can't remember it'; 'I felt very, very depressed'. A further four people described related feelings: one woman spoke of being 'perpetually exhausted'; another said:

> 'I was very emotionally broken at that time — I was feeling very
> sorry for myself; just about rock-bottom.' (105-F-47)

Another woman spoke of

'Having completely ground to a halt — wanting to give up. Physically
and emotionally I couldn't cope. I was always in tears.' (89-F-34)

A man described his feelings like this:

'A sort of general disorientation, really. I didn't know quite why I
was behaving as I was: a sort of general collapse of self-confidence.
I was looking in myself for something to cling onto, and finding
nothing at all. A great, gaping well.' (40-M-37)

Another kind of desolation that was repeatedly described was
associated with feelings of hopelessness: 'a sense that I was doomed to
failure'; 'a feeling of hopelessness and inability to alter my situation';
'a feeling of impotence'; 'despair and helplessness, that one could find
nothing to do about it'. One man felt 'trapped' by both his family and
his work situation, and a young woman spoke of angry frustration:
'I was beating my head against a brick wall — in many directions.'
Some felt passively, helplessly trapped; others responded angrily: 'I was
angry with myself and the rest of the world.' One woman was more
specific: 'I felt, I'm going to murder my husband if someone doesn't
help me.'

Six women said they felt 'suicidal', 'desperate'. One of these had
taken two overdoses within the previous year. Another described,

'an acute distress that I felt most of the time, and sometimes so
strongly that I was suicidal'. (87-F-31)

Another conveyed a strong sense that her life had seemed totally
purposeless and at risk:

'It was a matter of sheer physical survival — literally. The whole
matter, not just of living, but of existing'. (51-F-32)

A man described his suicidal impulses, and feelings of 'inferiority and
rage'.

The desperate feelings took the form of fear in several cases. Four
women spoke of a generalised fear: 'I was terrified of everything'; 'I was
frightened.' One person was more specific: 'It's very frightening to
know that things could get hold of you to such a degree.' She described
acute attacks of panic and fear, 'like falling down a cliff', and she was
afraid that, in that state, she might harm someone. Some other people
spoke of having felt very confused: 'I was in total confusion and
conflict'; 'I was in a turmoil, very confused.'

Two people described feelings of unbearable loneliness; another
spoke of insecurity, and four of acute anxiety. Several people also
referred to 'stress' and 'tension'. There were also two instances of
people having their distress compounded by feeling guilty because they
felt so bad. A further group, of seven women, described a complete loss
of self-confidence — they could think of no area of their lives in which

they felt competent or effective: 'I felt not good enough, as a mother, as a woman'; 'I had a completely negative image of myself'.

Difficulties in relationships

We have seen that many people defined their main problem, at the time of their approaching the Isis Centre, in terms of the distressing feelings they were experiencing then. The next largest category of problems was related to difficulties in specific relationships: these were cited by 44 of the 52 people.

If we first consider problems arising with parents, we find that these were described by ten people, all of them women. Four of these related their problems to their relationships with both parents. One was very aware of her dependence on them, having lived at home all her life. Now, at the age of thirty-one, she was trying to make an independent start. Another related difficulties with her husband to patterns established in her own childhood home: 'I had a long-standing feeling of having to earn approval: this was affecting my marriage'. A young woman in her twenties had returned from abroad to live in the same city as her parents, with whom she had had many conflicts. She spoke of having to 'come to terms with involvement with my family'. Another described herself as experiencing

'a conflict of values: wanting on the one hand to succeed by the standards set by my parents, and on the other hand to reject them totally. I was fluctuating between these positions, unable to establish my own mean'. (24-F-21)

Three other young women defined their problems as relating particularly to their relationships with their fathers. In each case there had been a very intense and ambivalent relationship during adolescence, which had not been resolved. This was now interfering with their making new, sexual relationships. Three more young women located their problems in their relationships with their mothers. In one case this was in the form of anxiety for her 'elderly and incapacitated mother, and her financial problems'; in the other two cases it was to do with conflicts remaining from very involved and complicated relationships as they grew up.

The largest group of relationship problems was that concerned with marital difficulties. These were given as being among their main problems by twenty people: seven men, nine women, and two married couples, who chose to work together on their difficulties. Nine of the individual people were trying to recover from the breakdown of their marriages, and seven were attempting to cope with and perhaps improve unsatisfactory situations. One of the couples presented a specifically sexual problem.

A further six people related their problems to difficulties in relationships with girl- and boyfriends. For four of these people the problem was to understand the reasons for the breakdown of such a relationship, to express the feelings involved and endure the loss; for the other two the dilemmas concerned assessing and making decisions about relationships that were continuing. Three further people were experiencing difficulties in relationships with colleagues at work.

The final group of specific relationship problems was that concerning children. Three women and one man (all in their forties and fifties) said that one of their main problems was their relationship with their adolescent or grown-up children. They voiced their regrets about their up-bringing; anxieties for them in adolescence or as married people; and difficulties in accepting their independence. Only one woman mentioned as a primary problem her relationship with her young children.

We have seen that a large group of people located their problems in a specific relationship, either in the difficulties of maintaining it or of enduring its loss. A further nine people cited relationships in general as constituting their main problem. They included three women and six men; of these, all but one of the men were in their early twenties; of the women, one was twenty-two, and both the others thirty-one. One of the latter said, 'I had difficulty in forming a relationship with anybody.' For a variety of reasons, from self-consciousness and anxiety to irritability or excessive dependence, they all had difficulty in 'getting on with people'; 'forming relationships'; 'establishing and maintaining personal relationships'.

Three other people, two women and one man, were frightened by the degree to which they had withdrawn from the struggle to make and sustain relationships: they cited their resultant isolation as a major source of worry.

'At that time I hated being on my own, even though I lived alone, but my state of mind seemed to keep me isolated. I felt self-conscious and strained with other people, as if I were posing.' (87-F-31)

Work and study problems

Another considerable group of problems related to working or studying. Fifteen people identified at least one of their main problems as being in this area. Seven of these were students, of whom four were undergraduates and three were postgraduates. Their difficulties included 'anxiety and depression' about their work; 'oppressive indecisiveness'; 'an inability to decide things or commit myself to anything'; difficulties in concentrating. Two students cited problems concerning some kind of emotional block which prevented them from being intuitive or emotionally expressive in relation to their work. One of these was a music student, concerned that his playing was 'styled accurate but uninvolved'; the other spoke of,

'a total failure of intuition and normal emotional responses, causing a feeling of social incompetence and an inability to criticise literature (I am taking an English degree), as well as deep depression'. (2-M-20)

Of the eight people who cited their jobs as the source of some of their problems, four were teachers, one teaching English as a foreign language, and the others teaching at a school, a polytechnic and a university respectively; one was an educational writer; one was employed in a publishing firm; one worked in a nursery and one was a supervisor in a shop. They complained variously of 'a job that I hated'; 'insecurity'; 'pressure of work'; demotion, diminishing satisfaction, acute anxiety; a 'general collapse of self-confidence', and 'unhappiness with the job I was in, and a lot of tension where I worked'.

A further six people, all women, said their main problem concerned their inability to cope with everyday tasks. One said she 'couldn't cope with running the home', another that she couldn't cope with things that cropped up. They found themselves feeling tearful and ineffective:

'A sense of being overwhelmed by the tasks I had to fulfil in everyday life.' (24-F-21)

Physical problems and specific symptoms

Another group of problems, cited by ten women and one man, was that related to their physical health, or to particular symptoms. Two spoke quite generally: 'my physical health cracked', 'my health was not good', and one related her symptoms to the menopause. Another complained of bodily pain and fatigue caused by a combination of physical problems. Another spoke of being 'very tense – using a lot of tranquillisers', and two described severe physical symptoms associated with anxiety states. One young man complained of 'nervous tension; I was all shaky for no reason'. He suffered extreme anxiety attacks, at work, for example, or when out shopping. One person had a phobia about eating; another suffered from agoraphobia. Another, who had some physical difficulties associated with her pregnancy, for which she was receiving special medical care, was also experiencing incapacitating phobic symptoms. Another woman was frightened by her own alarming behaviour: 'screaming – out of control'.

One person, a man, identified his problem as anxiety about his sexual identity. Four other people spoke of the financial problems they were having at the time. 'I had no work, friends, strength or money.'

To return to our initial hypothesis, that many people experience severe emotional distress, which they do not think of as medical in nature: these responses leave little doubt as to the intensity of the disturbing feelings experienced by those who came for counselling. In all but a few cases the emphasis was laid on problems of feeling, relating and daily living, and, where physical symptoms did exist, either relevant treatment was already being provided elsewhere, or the client recognised that there was some connection between his bodily symptoms and his psychological state, and it was this connection that he wanted to understand.

Why now?

In the previous section I gathered together the descriptions that people gave of the problems which led them to seek help. In many cases it was clear that these were not new problems but ones that had been troubling them for some time. Since our clients choose their own time for taking steps to deal with their problems, it is important to understand what finally determines them to do so. Possibilities include: the unhappy feelings growing so intense that they demand an outlet and can no longer be denied; or a particular event that finally dislodges a precarious system of defences; or a manifestation of the underlying problem that at last seems to justify a request for help. For example, in our culture, it may seem more familiar and more legitimate to seek help for distress expressed by a physical symptom, than for that which is experienced directly as an emotional state. The choice of a particular moment for seeking help – the answer to the question 'Why now?' – is important in that it clarifies for the counsellor the nature of the pressure on the client and something of his own view of his troubles. It also provides a starting point for linking his current distress to his general patterns of adaptation and, particularly, to similar critical times that he may have experienced before.

To determine first whether clients did indeed tend to view their problems as local, circumscribed events, or as related to long-established difficulties, they were asked to say when they felt they began. Each client was asked whether he felt his problems were of very recent onset (i.e. had begun in the last week or two before he came to the Isis Centre); or of fairly recent onset (i.e. had begun in the last few months); or had started within the previous year; or were long-standing.

Of the 52 people asked, 45 said their problems were long-standing. Of these, nine added some descriptive comment:

'I had had periods of depression for some years.' (26-F-22)
'I had gone up and down over the previous four or five years.' (90-F-37)
'Of about seven years' duration.' (24-F-21)

'My anxiety and depression were long-standing, from the age of ten or eleven.' (80-F-30)

Four people described 'long-standing' marital problems out of which a current crisis had developed. One woman spoke of hostility which had recently 'intensified to a murderous pitch'; another described a feeling of crisis precipitated by a particular incident involving her husband's rage. Five further people described long-standing difficulties which had been exacerbated during the previous year.

Forty-five people, then, spoke of their problems as long-standing. Of the remainder, five described the onset of their difficulties as 'within the previous year'; one felt they were 'of fairly recent onset'; and one came in as a result of a 'crisis within the last twenty-four hours'.

As with the answers to all the questions, one must remember that the client was speaking many months after the time he was describing. It is clear that his answers are likely to be influenced by many factors, among them being the effects of the counselling process itself. This particular one, concerning the onset of distress, is especially likely to have been so influenced, and we do not know how a client would have replied had he been asked this question when he came in. Later he is likely to have considered with his counsellor the connections between his current problem and previous experiences, and to have placed it in the context of his life as a whole. A result one might expect would be his then considering his troubles to be part of an intelligible pattern rather than a sudden and incomprehensible storm. Nevertheless, in spite of this possibility, we are entitled to believe that clients did feel their problems to be, in the main, deep-rooted, and pervasive in effect. We went on to ask the following question:

'What made you choose that particular time to seek some help?'

It is of particular interest to observe whether people more usually ascribe their impulse to seek help to the occurrence of a specific problem or crisis in the external world, or to the existence of an internal state of affairs that feels to be unendurable. Relevant thera-peutic styles that might be offered in response range in emphasis from a problem-centred, crisis-intervention model, through different degrees and forms of support, to a psycho-dynamic approach to experiences in the person's inner world.

Feelings

In thinking back to the point in time when they first sought help, many clients again recalled the frightening and distressing feelings they were experiencing then:

'I felt quite desperate.' (128-F-33)
'I just felt at the bottom of the pit.' (88-F-30)
'It was so frightening.' (91-F-34)
'I felt everything had got out of proportion and I needed some external help.' (54-F-26)
'The stress had just become unbearable.' (39-M-32)

For many people it is hard both to admit that someone else's help may be needed, and to feel entitled to ask for that help.

'I had been unhappy for some time. I gradually dropped my iron rule that I must at all costs resolve the thing on my own' (24-F-21).

Some people had retreated from others:

'I had had several weeks of feeling very tense, tearful, depressed — not wanting to see people.' (90-F-37)
'I was conscious of being very lonely.' (108-F-51)
'I felt quite desperate to talk to someone.' (68-F-32)

One man felt very much alone and was afraid of his own thoughts. One woman felt that her internal state of fear was becoming visible:

'People were staring at me: this is what it felt like.' (53-F-35)

Others found that the intensity of their feelings was affecting them in other ways:

'I had recently had long spells of weeping, and of standing motionless, indecisively.' (54-F-26)
'I was getting pretty snappy.' (95-M-47)
'My anxiety was so great that it was threatening my work.' (41-M-32)

Another person was finding that her anxiety expressed itself in the form of physical symptoms:

'I was losing sense of time and place; forgetting to breathe; having palpitations.' (128-F-33)

Fifteen people in all responded to the question of 'why now?' in terms of the intensity of the feelings involved, and the threat they posed to their ability to cope with everyday life. It seems that these people were prompted to act in response to considerations that were primarily located within rather than outside themselves.

Turning points in relationships, and other experiences of loss and change

An almost equal number of people related their decision to seek help to life events, usually involving loss or distressing change. We have seen that among the most frequently presented problems are difficulties in relationships. The moment of choosing to seek some help had often been determined by some kind of crisis within an already troubled relationship:

> 'My wife disclosed that she was having an affair.' (5-M-25)
> 'My husband had finally decided to go and live with someone else
> — after about eighteen months of uncertainty.' (89-F-34)
> 'The problem with my wife came to a head.' (97-M-43)

Six people had come in because of crises within their marriage. Similarly, seven people were acutely distressed because of breaking-up with a girl- or boyfriend.

> 'This was the most recent in a very long train of disasters with boyfriends'. (69-F-30)

This might have been a very recent event, or one which had occurred earlier but left distress that would not heal.

> 'I had broken with my girlfriend six months previously — this seemed to get more and more magnified.' (4-M-23)

For one woman, separation from a man she had loved was compounded by the death of a close woman-friend.

For two other people, the feelings of loss and of being abandoned were associated with a more general movement of friends away from Oxford. One mentioned the impact of her friends leaving; the other said:

> 'Most of my close friends had, within a short space of time, left the area, and I was suddenly devoid of people to talk seriously to. I was, therefore, bottling up problems.' (68-F-32)

Another man had been overwhelmed with loneliness when his daughter left home and he had to live alone. He was divorced from his wife and had brought up his daughter on his own.

> 'It was an overwhelming sense of loneliness, I think. My one and only daughter had got married a few months previously. There was a terrific vacuum when she left. I hadn't expected this — it got unbearable.' (96-M-49)

Even when the loss of an important relationship was not mentioned by a client as having been among his main problems, it can be seen that it was often (i.e. in sixteen cases) a major precipitating factor in seeking help.

Associations have, of course, been found in other settings between experiences of loss and change, and the onset of severe mental distress (Brown and Harris, 1978; Marris, 1974; Parkes, 1972). We have cited many examples of the loss or disruption of relationships as experienced by our clients. We do also find examples of disorientation and loss of confidence due to changes of circumstances. Four people mentioned 'moving house' , 'coming to Oxford', 'coming to Oxford and living on my own', 'moving into new digs', as factors which added to their burden of stress sufficiently to lead them to seek help.

At the suggestion of someone else

I have emphasised that the Isis Centre operates on the basis of clients referring themselves; that is, they do not come at the behest of anyone else, and they are responsible for deciding whether what is offered there can be of use to them. They make their own arrangements accordingly with a counsellor. Nevertheless, the first information that the Centre exists, and some description of what happens there, often comes from another person, sometimes professional, sometimes private. Eighteen people mentioned that someone telling them about the Centre, or suggesting that they might come, was among their reasons for coming when they did.

Eight people had decided to come when they heard of the Isis Centre from a professional source: four from their doctors; two from the Family Planning Association; one from the adolescent unit of a local hospital; one from a former therapist elsewhere. Three others had friends who had some professional knowledge of the Isis Centre and had suggested it as a resource. Three other people had responded to recommendations from the Samaritans that they might come.

The remaining four people had heard the work of the Isis Centre described by friends and had decided to come. All these people conveyed the impression that they had been searching for a resource of this kind and were very relieved to find it.

Other reasons

There were a number of other reasons given by people for their choice of a particular time for approaching the Isis Centre. One that was shared by several people was exasperation with other forms of help. One woman felt that she had exhausted the possibilities of medical resources, and another said:

'I had seen my GP, who was no help at all. I had also seen a
psychiatrist, and had a two week stay in hospital. No practical
help or advice was offered — just drugs. I was very reluctant to take
these because I did not feel that they in any way solved the
problem.' (80-F-30)

Another person said she had determined to give up the antidepressant tablets that she had taken for some years, and a young man declared:

'It sort of came to a head. I went to the doctor – he just gave me tablets – they made me feel even more weird. If they didn't work, he didn't bother.' (7-M-23)

Three people linked their decision to seek help at that time with stress associated with their work. One said he was responding to tension and dissatisfaction that had slowly built up. Two others, who were both teachers, had come in in the autumn: 'a bad time of year'. They had each felt the stress of the new academic year approaching.

One man who, in his capacity as a helper in a voluntary agency, had sometimes recommended others to come, decided to take his own advice. Others came for reasons including: anxiety about someone else's health; isolation that he could bear no longer; and 'financial problems – and the endless problems of a one-parent family'.

In the opening chapter, I observed that there are many familiar forms of distress which are powerful enough to overwhelm a person, and to distort or halt the natural development of his life. These may have their origin in very early experiences of deprivation or distorted relationships, or may develop later, at any time when someone encounters difficulties which exceed his capacity for constructive response, and which force him into strategies of defence. What the people in our study report so vividly are the painful feelings that accompany such experiences, and which are frightening in themselves because of their force and unfamiliarity.

Many of their accounts strikingly resemble those of participants in other recent interview studies, such as those by Eric Sainsbury (1975) and by Anthony Maluccio (1979). Maluccio writes, of people coming to a family service agency:

As clients talked about their presenting problems, their descriptions reflected a common theme of desperation and confusion . . . .
There were indications that the search for outside help was typically triggered not so much by a specific event, as by the feeling that the situation had become intolerable and that the client had no-one else to turn to.

He notes the similarities of his findings to those of studies concerning the approach to mental health agencies.

In describing the immediate reasons for their distressing feelings, our clients consistently associate them with dilemmas and conflicts arising in their family, social and working lives. Freud, when asked what he thought a normal person should be able to do well, is said to have replied: to love and to work. It is precisely in these areas that our clients locate their problems, and in these areas too, as we shall see in the following chapter, that they hope for constructive change.

The difficulties are naturally defined in terms of feelings and of relationships. Earlier I suggested that to describe these kinds of experience in terms that assume they are akin to physical illnesses, and to set about treating them in a similar way, tends both to obscure them and to hinder their solution. Thomas Szasz (1970) argues that:

> we have failed to accept the simple fact that human relations are inherently fraught with difficulties, and to make them even relatively harmonious requires much patience and hard work. . . . My aim . . . is to suggest that the phenomena now called mental illnesses be looked at afresh and more simply, that they be removed from the category of illnesses, and that they be regarded as the ` expressions of man's struggle with the problem of how he should live.

Chapter 5

Clients' hopes and expectations

As we have seen, one of the special characteristics of the Isis Centre is that people can, if they wish, choose to come to it directly, without any intervening negotiation with a doctor or other professional person. One consequence of this is that the counsellors must be prepared to respond to people with an extremely wide range of problems, and with very varied expectations as to what may be provided.

For some people this is the first time in their lives that they have undertaken to seek help with private, personal problems. Among them are some who have puzzled alone for a long while and have formed in their minds a very distinct idea as to what another person could contribute. There are others who have never imagined themselves in this role, but feel precipitated into it by some unexpected upheaval in their lives. They feel suddenly unable to manage without help but have no idea what form that help might take.

Others again have already had experience of treatment of one form or another for their emotional difficulties. Sometimes they feel grateful for the help they have received and are seeking something further that will be akin to it. Sometimes they have felt baulked and frustrated, and they are searching for something quite different. Overall, the hopes and expectations of the people who come to the Isis Centre vary very widely, and they range from the completely vague to the dogmatically precise.

Self-referral or 'walk-in' mental health centres have been developed further in the United States than in Britain. Lazare (1975) and his colleagues, particularly, have studied the implications of an unselected clientele, presenting with a complex range of problems and a very heterogeneous collection of expectations and requests. They have developed what they describe as the 'customer approach', in which careful attention is paid to the specific requests made by each patient. They stress that therapists working in conventional clinics customarily

45

take heed of the patient's complaints and of his goals in seeking treatment, but are less careful in ascertaining the kind of help he is asking for. They see this as one of the essential elements in the preliminary negotiations between therapist and patient, and one which, if properly handled, may provide the basis for an understanding that will allow useful work to take place. It may be that the client has his heart set on a form of intervention that the clinic simply cannot provide, or that the therapist judges to be inappropriate or undesirable. If this is the case it is important that it be clarified as soon as possible, so that they may then explore whether there is an alternative possibility, acceptable to and valued by both parties. If this is not the case it is still preferable for this to be ascertained, and, for example, information provided as to alternative, more appropriate resources.

One of the most important reasons for taking care that the client has the opportunity to explain what he is seeking is that it necessitates his being and feeling heard. His viewpoint is respected, and it is included in the decision-making process in which both he and the therapist are involved, with the aim of concluding whether they can usefully work together. It may be, of course, that the client has not consciously formulated his hopes and wishes on seeking help, but being invited to do so can be the first step towards the clarification of his view of his problems.

Since this mode of thinking is clearly relevant to work in the early sessions of a client's contact with the Isis Centre, we included two related questions in the follow-up interview. In the first we asked about the client's goals in seeking help: that is, what he had hoped to change or achieve by coming to the Isis Centre. In the second of these questions we asked in what way he hoped someone at the Centre might be able to help him achieve his goals.

'What did you hope to accomplish for yourself when you came to the Isis Centre? What sort of things did you hope to change or achieve?'

Answers to this question fall into four main groups: those recording hopes of *change in feelings*, relief from distressing emotional states, and increase in self-esteem and confidence; those referring to hopes of *gaining greater understanding*, both of self and of the problems to be dealt with; those which expressed hopes of *regaining an ability to cope with life*, and to be able to work effectively again; and those involving hopes of *improvement in relationships*. Some clients expressed hopes of change in more than one of these areas.

Change in feelings

If we look first at the group who emphasised a wish for some change in their feelings, we find that 22 of the 52 clients mentioned a desire of this kind. They hoped, for example, for 'a relief of troubles in all contexts' or 'relief from distress'; 'the relief of talking about it'. Sometimes this was a desperate hope, without much confidence that relief would be possible.

'I don't think I had any hopes. It was probably sheer desperation. I had no idea what *could* come out of it. Almost: nothing worse can happen, so try.' (51-F-32)
'I don't think I even thought about that — I was just desperate.' (69-F-30)
'I had no idea what the outcome would be. Perhaps the load might become lighter — "a trouble shared is a trouble halved"?' (96-M-49)

One person felt that, if she were to experience some relief, she must change

'everything! I needed to stop feeling so bad.' (26-F-22)

Others said:

'I don't think I expected much. I just *had* to talk to somebody.' (106-F-43)
'I just wanted to be normal again — to get rid of the troubling feelings.' (7-M-23)

Some people were specific about hoping for relief from depression:

'I would have liked not to be depressed.' (98-M-54)
'I really wanted immediate alleviation of my depression, and perhaps I hoped I could get to know myself more.' (79-F-32)

One woman gave her aim in coming as:

'I hoped to have support while I tried doing without the antidepressant tables.' (107-F-48)

One man hoped for change in the anxious feelings and symptoms of both himself and his wife:

'It's difficult to specify . . . what I hoped to achieve was the removal or alleviation of [wife's] anxieties — and the prospering of our relationship. I also hoped that the symptoms of my own anxieties would be dealt with and helped.' (127-M-38)

This man's wife expressed her hopes for change in related terms, seeking to allay her fears for herself and her husband:

'I feared that I was going out of my mind. . . . I was worried that there was something radically wrong with me. I was also burying the fear that my husband was seriously ill himself.' (128-F-33)

One woman said she hoped to become more confident:

'I was hoping that I would develop more faith in myself.' (78-F-35)

Others said:

'I needed to be more steady and straight.' (27-F-23)
'I felt as though I had lost everything – I didn't exist any more.
I needed to confirm my existence.' (91-F-34)

The particular feelings that one man hoped to change were those of acute self-consciousness in social situations.

There is striking consistency in the way in which people emphasise their feelings, in accounting for seeking help at all, in giving a reason for coming at a particular time, and in terms of what they hoped to change. This underlines the central importance of the counsellor hearing these feelings accurately, facilitating their expression, and giving the client the experience of being really heard.

Gaining greater understanding

Another group of people described their hopes for change in more cognitive terms. They said that what they wanted to achieve was some understanding, and perhaps resolution, of the complexities of their feelings, motives or behaviour. They sought to clarify their problems and perhaps find solutions to their dilemmas. Seventeen people spoke of aims of this kind, as illustrated by the following quotations:

'I wanted to reach an understanding, and some sort of resolution,
of my emotional state.' (6-M-25)
'I hoped to achieve some clarity about what I was doing; to
understand why I had done it before, why I was likely to do it
again.' (66-F-29)

This client was speaking particularly of what she saw as a pattern of committing herself to 'frustrating, dead-end relationships' with men.

'Understanding. I wanted to find reasons for my problem and a
means of remedying it – at least, to be better adjusted.' (3-M-23)
'I hoped to learn more about myself and the reasons for what I
felt were problems holding me back from self-development.'
(110-F-41)
'I suppose to try and find out more about what had gone wrong;
to get to the roots of the problem.' (70-F-28)
'I really wanted to find out why I was behaving as I was – and,
if possible, to use that knowledge to change the behaviours and
attitudes in myself that I didn't like. I wanted to find something

to hold onto in myself — some identity. This was something I was quite unsure of.

'I wanted to want to go back to my wife and children — but this was pointless unless some sort of change had taken place. But I needed to know the root causes of this "identity crisis", "moral crisis", before change could take place.' (40-M-37)

This man was stressing the wish both to understand and to translate that understanding into some form of constructive change. This was echoed by three other clients:

'I hoped I could (I knew the causes) — I hoped I could *do* something about it. I wanted to come and understand, so I could do it for myself — and not need propping up.' (88-F-30)
'I hoped to gain a little more understanding of my problems, and, hopefully, then be able to handle them more successfully.' (68-F-32)
'I suppose I hoped to change myself, knowing from previous experience that only by changing my own attitudes could I improve my life again.' (87-F-31)

As we have seen, in considering the troubling states of mind in which people approach the Centre, confusion is one of those repeatedly described. It is not surprising then, that clarification of problems is a goal stressed by many clients.

'Things had become very confused — I was not sure I could see the problems clearly.' (128-F-33)
'I was doing an enormous amount of thinking on my own, but not sharing it with anyone. . . . I wanted to talk to someone systematically — trying to put my thoughts together somehow.' (1-M-21)
'Perhaps, initially, to get my thoughts and ideas sorted out; get calm; get things into perspective . . . I was in such a muddle — a clinging to straws.' (67-F-28)
'I wanted to see if there was something in me that was distorting things. Possibly to clarify the whole situation. Were there decisions I should take?' (90-F-37)

Two people had hoped specifically that understanding their situation better would enable them to solve the dilemmas they were in, and suggest a way forward.

'Hard to say — I did not believe it would have any magic key, but I suppose I hoped for encouragement to break out of the work/ family "double bind".' (95-M-47)
'I was hoping that I'd be able to reach a decision.' (78-F-35)

For this woman, this involved a choice between staying with her husband, or leaving him for someone else.

Regaining an ability to cope with life and to work effectively

The stress in the preceding answers tends to be on understanding and clarifying the situation, sometimes in the expectation that this would lead to change. Others (eleven people) were primarily concerned with their everyday activities and commitments, and hoped to regain their ability to deal with these satisfactorily.

'I wanted to start coping with life again.' (128-F-33)
'I wanted to get back to normal; to be able to do my work and get on with people normally again; knowing what to say, how to behave.' (2-M-20)
'I just wanted to cope with everyday living.' (109-F-54)

One woman was particularly seeking a solution to her problem of agoraphobia, in the hope of being able to resume a more normal way of life:

'I hoped to find some way of overcoming my agoraphobia, or at least a way of learning to accept it. . . . I hoped to achieve more independence, and to be able to move towards going out alone.' (80-F-30)

For several people anxieties about their work were predominant.

'I wanted to become productive at my work.' (54-F-26)
'I hoped to obtain some advice, about how I might cope better with anxiety — particularly in lecturing situations.' (41-M-32)
'The immediate thing: to help me to get through my studies with less emotional distress.' (25-F-22)
'Perhaps to be able to stay in my job.' (67-F-28)

Another woman stressed her wish to be able to work again, but this also clearly stood for a wider regaining of confidence and self-respect.

'I wanted to . . . get back my self-confidence and self-respect sufficiently to work again, and to restore what had been a good and creative, out-going relationship with myself and others.' (104-F-48)

Among her problems was one concerning eating, a phobic difficulty in swallowing. She explained what a solution to this problem would mean to her life as a whole:

'To be able to eat normally would mean the end of several problems: the personal anguish, the isolation, the shame, the loss of weight and strength, so that I could be "normal" and work, and go out for fun as other people did and as I used to do.' (104-F-48)

This idea of regaining 'normality', a familiar way of living that seems to resemble the experience of others in a reassuring way, was also expressed by another person.

'I hoped for miracles. I hoped I could be restored to what I thought was normal; the condition in which I'd spent forty years of my life.' (106-F-43)

Improvement in relationships

Another aim described by a number of people involved improvement in relationships, sometimes general, sometimes specific.

'I hoped to be able to talk to someone about my being not very good in my relations with other people. . . . To give me an understanding of my situation, and a better outlook on my relationships with people, and my understanding of others.' (52-F-33)
'I wanted to change the feeling of constant anxiety with people; to find out what was actually happening.' (4-M-23)

One woman described a desire to improve relationships with others as part of a general wish to enter into life more fully and more positively:

'I wanted to function at full capacity; to commit myself fully to people and to work and tasks; to stop struggling *against* things (parents, authority, obligations) and start struggling *for* things. I wanted to relax, feel comfortable with people, and to be able to take in information and details, instead of always worrying that I was doing something wrong.' (24-F-21)

Another person hoped for change in her relationships with men particularly.

'I wanted to see if there was anything I could do about not messing up relationships generally — with men. I seemed to be always too demanding; terribly anxious to have someone to share things with, and yet fiercely independent.' (90-F-37)

One other woman wanted to clarify her relationship with her father, and solve some of the dilemmas it posed now he was elderly and ill.

Six people came to the Isis Centre in the hope of achieving some changes within their marriages. A man already quoted had spoken of a wish for the 'prospering of our relationship' as an outcome of the alleviation of his and his wife's anxieties. Another man said that his primary reason for coming was 'Some hope of a salvage operation (for his marriage) at first'. In fact he describes how his goals changed a bit as he went on:

51

'After three or four meetings, I started to be aware of my narrow perspective — and compartmentalisation of emotions. Then I sought to change — no, that's too strong. But I was prepared to be adventurous, to explore while I was here.' (5-M-25)

Another man described a similar change in his goals. At first he had hoped to:

'Get guidance on possible ways to attempt to salvage our marriage. When this failed, I wanted to learn more about myself and why this relationship failed, so as to avoid making the same mistakes again.' (39-M-32)

Others said:

'I wanted to make it possible for my marriage to continue.' (6-M-25)
'I hoped to understand (husband's) temperament, and the way I react to it.' (105-F-47)

A married couple who came together sought:

'A return to our original good experience of sex.' (129-M-23 and 130-F-22)

This summarises what clients said they had hoped to change or achieve when they came to the Isis Centre; the next section describes the kinds of help they said they were hoping for, to achieve these ends.

'In what way or ways did you hope that the Centre might be able to help you?'

The responses to this question fall into five main groups. Some people expressed much *uncertainty* as to what might be expected. Others stressed that they had looked forward simply to *talking to someone*. This also involved variously: a need to be released from isolation; an opportunity to be open and unguarded with someone not personally involved in the situation; or a request for an objective response. A third group of people emphasised their hope of gaining *psychological insight* into their difficulties, a way of understanding better what they were experiencing. Others again were seeking *advice*, and others various forms of *support*.

Uncertainty

Asked to indicate the sort of help they had expected at the Isis Centre, several people stressed that they had no clear idea at the time as to what was either desirable or possible. In several cases the Isis Centre had seemed like a last resort; people had come in despair, without a clearly formulated expectation as to what would follow, for instance:

'I didn't know what I'd find.' (1-M-21)
'I didn't know, but I knew I couldn't keep on alone.' (77-F-33)
'I didn't have any ideas or hopes; I was in despair.' (91-F-34)
'I didn't hope for anything. One thing I did think: it's someone else's problem as well now – it's going to be shared. The problem had been going on for so long.' (69-F-30)
'I didn't really know. I knew I'd have to talk about it first of all – I didn't know how it would go from there.' (7-M-23)

One woman said she had not known what kind of help she was seeking, but did have some fears as to what might be offered.

'What I was afraid of was – you know, you hear of people going back and back and back in their lives – I didn't want to do that.' (109-F-54)

She spoke of the 'onion' image: stripping off layer after layer until there is nothing left. She said she was suspicious of 'delving', as being 'too introspective and time-consuming'.

Another person was aware that he had come with very contradictory hopes: wanting to be independent and yet longing for someone else to take over.

'I was probably expecting far too much of the other person, being able to do it for me. I was aware of the contradictions: I *must* do it myself; someone must make it possible.' (4-M-23)

Talking to someone

Many people said that their main need was 'to talk to someone', and some stressed the particular qualities they wanted that person to have. Those who spoke more generally said:

'I desperately needed to talk to someone. I had a problem I had never discussed with anyone – I had mainly refused to discuss it with myself.' (96-M-49)
'I had some expectation of communication; with the possibility of its being on-going.' (66-F-29)
'I just felt I had to discuss seemingly overwhelming problems with well-adjusted people.' (68-F-32)
'Just talking mainly – to people who understand.' (53-F-35)
'I simply thought I'd be able to talk and get some response from a professional of some sort.' (25-F-22)
'Talking to someone about relationships.' (52-F-33)

These people have mentioned the hope of talking with someone 'well-adjusted', 'understanding' and 'professional'. Several others emphasised the importance of talking to someone who would offer objectivity and detachment:

> 'I hoped to find someone with whom I was not emotionally
> involved, to go through my situation.' (95-M-47)
> 'I wanted someone who knew nothing about me previously – who
> could offer professional detachment. This is easier than talking to
> friends.' (67-F-28)
> 'Perhaps talking to someone detached from all the turmoil could
> help?' (91-F-34)
> 'I knew from (hospital) experience that it would be good to talk
> to some quite objectively.' (108-F-51)
> 'Someone to look at things objectively, dispassionately.' (89-F-34)

Others said that they had wanted to talk to someone with whom it
would be possible to be completely open and unguarded.

> 'I wanted freedom to expose the whole problem – to make a more
> rounded decision; to get out of the fog. I wanted to be able to
> drop the coping front.' (67-F-28)
> 'I assumed I'd be able to tell someone absolutely frankly about
> this problem – I had otherwise been ashamed to do so.' (108-F-51)

One woman said she had hoped for help of two different kinds, the one
leading on from the other:

> 'Partly I just wanted some all-understanding semi-anonymous
> mother-confessor, to whom I could pour out my tale of woe. I
> thought if I could tell it in this way I would understand the
> problems better, through having to bring them out into the open
> and explain them.
> 'Then I hoped the counsellor would help me to get to the root
> of the problems, especially since I felt there were things I was
> ignoring, and could not bear to admit or accept. I thought the
> counsellor would help by asking me questions, probing.' (24-F-21)

Psychological insight

The second half of the previous answer is akin to those of people who
said they wanted to talk to someone who would offer and encourage
insight into problems, and understanding of feelings, motives and
behaviour. They sought help in understanding themselves as a first step
towards dealing with their problems.

> 'Basically we expected to talk. . . . We felt a need to understand
> what was going wrong for us.' (129-M-23 and 130-F-25)
> 'Help in understanding myself.' (6-M-25)
> 'Insight from counselling about deeper understanding of the
> mechanisms of intimate personal relationships; how and why

people (couples) interact in the ways they do.' (39-M-32)
'I thought that someone who was experienced and knowledgeable
about such things would guide me to a better understanding of
myself.' (110-F-41)
'I thought that, if (my problem) were caused by some emotional
block or newly revived trauma, that that would be spotted and,
under guidance, I could come to terms with it.' (2-M-20)
'I hoped to be able to get help sorting through the hopeless maze
of things that seemed to be wrong in my life, and find a way to
begin tackling them.' (77-F-33)

In several instances those who described in psychological terms the
kind of help they were seeking were basing their expectations on some
previous experience of therapy. Sometimes they were now seeking a
contrast, sometimes something similar. For example, a woman who had
experience of co-counselling was now looking for something rather
different:

'I knew it would be counselling help — I now wanted guidance
and insight. Someone to help pick things out — the opposite of a
peer thing. . . . I had some feeling of wanting someone else to take
the reins.' (89-F-34)

One woman was basing her expectations on her husband's former
experience:

'I thought it would involve discussion, rather than drugs or any
physical treatment. I didn't know what particular technique would
be used. My husband's experience at [hospital] had focused on
childhood experiences. I had something like that in my mind.'
(128-F-33)

Another based her ideas of what might be helpful on talks she had had
with her doctor:

'I had had experience from my G.P. of fairly incisive remarks,
which were more helpful than sympathy.' (105-F-47)

In contrast to this, another woman had had difficulty in talking to
her doctor and had felt that he had not taken her seriously.

'I wanted to be able to speak without fear of being classed simply
"neurotic" and dismissed. . . . I wanted to be seen as myself.'
(104-F-48)

Two people said they had expected 'counselling'; one had had some
sessions at the Isis Centre before, and the other had been to the
University Counselling Service. She amplified her answer:

'I wanted somebody to talk to; who would understand and share,
and help me sort out something (but I didn't know what).' (27-F-23)

She had particularly hoped for help with a marital sexual problem, or
referral on for this. One other person said he had expected 'Counselling
— or possibly a referral.'

Two further people related their expectations, even if quite vague, to
former experience:

'I imagined it would be something like psychiatric help I'd had
before. I didn't want a group; I didn't expect to have answers; I
didn't really know.' (90-F-37)
'I had seen a psychotherapist recently — I thought it might be less
firmly based in a particular school here, but I expected something
similar.' (26-F-22)

Advice

A number of people said that they had come to the Isis Centre in hope
of getting clear advice as to how to deal with their problems, or a new
method of approach.

'I just thought someone might be able to show me another way of
tackling the problem.' (56-F-27)
'With concrete advice.' (41-M-32)
'In discussing personal relationships . . . I hoped I could be helped
to accept what I couldn't change, or find a new approach to
resolve those I could . . . In discussing the eating phobia — the
extreme fear of actually swallowing — and the many ways I'd tried
to break this, I'd hoped for some new angle, something I'd
perhaps overlooked or was unaware of.' (104-F-48)

Some indicated disappointment as they replied in this way.

'I anticipated that it would be much as it was. I would have shied
away from group therapy or anything like that. I hoped, perhaps,
for more direct advice, as I was floundering from one choice to
another.' (78-F-35)
'I wanted someone to tell me what to do. I wanted someone to
justify the course of action I chose, e.g. at that time, leaving home.
I needed my confidence supported. . . . I kept saying to
[counsellor] : tell me what to do, from your wide experience.'
(97-M-43)

Others had come for advice of quite specific kinds:

'Advice as to whether psychoanalysis would be a good idea . . .
advice about psychiatrists, etc. . .' (3-M-23)
'I wanted advice as to how to persuade my father to seek treatment.

What was my position as his daughter? I didn't then have in mind the question of exploring the relationship.' (55-F-26)

Support

Some people, then, came in expectation òf receiving explicit advice; others stressed that they were seeking primarily support and reassurance.

'I wanted reassurance, at first.' (54-F-26)
'I was coming for support.' (90-F-37)

One woman was unsure as to what she most urgently hoped for:

'I had only vague ideas about how this (i.e. change for the better) could come about. I desperately wanted to talk to someone who would give me support, or insights, or advice . . . offering professional support and advice.' (87-F-31)

Another described her original wish for a kind of support in a wry tone:

'I was hoping to get a woman to sympathise with me against men.' (105-F-47)

She later described her feelings in responding to the challenge of finding herself talking with a young man.

Someone else envisaged the support more in terms of the structure of the counselling than the relationship.

'I felt it would be a help to know I was going to come here regularly, for a given length of time. A kind of insurance against the frightening thoughts becoming private again.' (1-M-21)

One woman was seeking support and the opportunity to share her thoughts particularly while she discontinued her medication:

'I thought discussing difficulties as they arose might enable me to do without the medication (which dulls the mind to some extent).' (107-F-48)

Another had had extensive experience of both hospitalisation and medication and was seeking a new kind of approach.

'I wanted to talk things over with someone, instead of being prescribed drugs and sent home.' (80-F-30)

Three people envisaged possible help in terms of someone strengthening their resolve to do things that were frightening and difficult, but seemed necessary. In one case this was in making a psychological effort; in the others it was more to do with external matters.

'I think what emerged . . . was a sort of fairly thick protective wall,
which I built around my inner self, which I feel is very vulnerable.
I think I was looking for someone to help me, encourage me, to
look over that wall.' (40-M-37)
'I hoped the Centre might strengthen my resolve or incentive, and
help push me into working.' (54-F-26)
'I thought I might be able to be more decisive with someone as
witness. Telling someone would support my resolution.' (90-F-37)

Another form of wished-for support was described in the following
terms:

'In a general sort of way I wanted to be validated by somebody.
The break-up had left me feeling I was wrong — out of touch with
other people's values. I wanted to be confirmed in some way — to
find a way back to my own view-point.' (65-F-31)

One other kind of help was described by a man who came with his wife
for conjoint sessions:

'I felt that what we needed was a third party to act as umpire,
referee, mediator, interlocutor.' (127-M-38)

When a person begins to work with a counsellor, it is clearly important that they together undertake that work with some agreement both
as to their goals and as to the process by which they expect to approach
them. Therapists who offer related forms of psychotherapy in other
settings, and who have evolved careful selection procedures for
choosing the people they work with, stress the importance of the
patient's motivation and expectations. Sifneos, in America, and Malan,
at the Tavistock Clinic in London, independently arrived at very similar
criteria for accepting people for brief psychotherapy. They include an
ability on the part of the patient to recognise that his symptoms are
psychological in origin, and a willingness to participate with the
therapist in exploring his difficulties. Suitable clients are thought to
share the therapist's primary goal of *understanding*, with the expectation that beneficial changes will occur in their lives as a result. Sifneos
(1979) looks for signs of motivation of this kind at the first meeting
with the patient; Malan (1976), as a result of his extended outcome
studies, suggests that the capacity to evolve such motivation relatively
early in the treatment may suffice, even if it is not evident right from
the start. The development of a shared ethos of this sort may indeed be
an early goal of the work.

We have looked at the answers given by clients to the questions
concerning their goals and hopes on approaching the Isis Centre.
What is very noticeable is the high proportion of people who are
consciously seeking help through talking, about problems which they

undoubtedly regard as psychological. Even when they formulate their goals in terms of changes in relationships and activities, again and again they emphasise that they expect such changes to come as a result of better understanding of their own feelings and attitudes. Straker (1968) has noted a high correlation between self-referral and favourable outcome to therapy, and at the Isis Centre, also, we see that the processes involved in self-referral often lead to people selecting themselves relevantly and bringing themselves to a resource which may indeed meet their needs.

We also find, however, that a substantial number of people came seeking support or advice, and that they were relying heavily on their counsellors to provide them with expert recommendations for dealing with their difficulties. Since the counsellors are committed to attempting to help people solve their own problems, it is clear that some initial negotiations must take place in such cases, in order for counsellor and client to clarify their roles in the sessions. If an acceptable balance cannot be found, it is likely that they will both experience frustration and disappointment. We go on now to look at clients' descriptions of such difficulties and the related negotiations.

Chapter 6

What happened in the sessions?

In the second chapter, I outlined some ideas and convictions, shared on the whole by the Isis Centre team, as to the nature and goals of the counselling relationship. We have also looked at clients' accounts of their hopes and expectations when they approached the Centre. We turn now to see, through the clients' eyes, what happened when these sets of expectations met.

As a rule, people described the verbal content of the sessions only in the most general terms. Most emphasised the discussion of current events and experiences: some indicated the usefulness of linking these to the past, others were in doubt as to the relevance of this. What emerged vividly was that the question of what to bring to the sessions was a puzzle for a significant number of people. This caused distress that seems, sometimes, to have been underestimated by the counsellors, or was certainly difficult to contain and solve within the relationship.

For many people this question presented no problems. They were urgent to express their feelings and talk about their difficulties: the provision of an opportunity to do this, and a receptive atmosphere, proved to be enough, especially at the beginning. Many people described an easy flow of material, with the counsellor in the role of listener, responding seriously and attentively, but rarely taking the initiative. The following quotations provide some examples:

'Bringing in events of the week, and reflecting on them. Trying to pin-point one's reactions — and to think how to cope with them. Trying to make some order from the jumble . . . Basically, I would sit, as now — and chatting. She would elicit the information. I would start on a free flow of what had happened. She would take up details of interest — a kind of analysis. It was a conversation — but she guided it, in a sense. There was some linking back to parents and to one's reactions to them, and relationships with them. It opened out — in terms of the things she picked out. [The counsellor] would sum up at the end of the session — would suggest some ideas to follow.' (67-F-28)

'It varied tremendously; sometimes I came very full of ideas and could talk, on my own, for an hour. Usually concerning the past — and patterns. Other times, I wanted to talk about current things — more narrative, less generalised. The counsellor was equally accepting of both kinds of material. She questioned me a bit, but generally let me do most of the talking.' (1-M-21)

'In the sessions I talked mostly about what happened during the week and my reactions to it. She would often ask questions and, rarely, now and again, make suggestions. It really amounted to telling my biography. The counsellor was a good listener, making occasional perceptive and enlightening comments.' (95-M-47)

The feeling of fluency and ease conveyed by these clients is in marked contrast with the frustration experienced by some others, who felt they had needed more active help from their counsellors, particularly in deciding what was relevant material to bring to the sessions. This was summed up by the woman who said:

'I could never see quite what we were trying to do. I'm supposed to sit and talk, and I don't know what to talk about.' (109-F-54)

Feeling a lack of guidance from their counsellors, some people tried earnestly to persevere, as though on their own:

'I endeavoured to examine myself and try to understand myself more fully. The counsellor listened and occasionally made comments — but much of the time I felt unable to get anywhere.' (110-F-41)

'I mostly just sat down and talked. I don't think I really knew what I was talking about. I tried desperately to put a structure round it.' (69-F-30)

Others began to consider the nature of this problem, the question of who was to be responsible for the sessions and their content.

'Initially, it was really nice, just to come along and talk to somebody. I was really grateful about that. Then I realised it was going to be up to me to decide and find out what I wanted from the sessions. This probably angered and confused me, but may have done me some good. I felt increasing annoyance that things seemed so one-sided...' (4-M-23)

The way in which this problem is solved may well be one of the crucial determinants of the outcome of counselling. The man just quoted felt increasingly angry and deprived, feeling that his counsellor abandoned him in the face of an insuperable problem.

'The counsellor had to take a distanced stance – this stopped me.
There was no feed-back to help me express myself. . . . I wish she
could have told me what she thought of me, of my coming.'
(4-M-23)

Others encountered the same turning-point, and were able, or were
enabled, to take a different path.

'My counsellor listened to whatever I wanted to talk about. I found
a disconcerting lack of continuity at times from session to session,
but I think that was because I wanted her to take more of a
leadership role and tell me what to do or talk about. In retrospect,
I think it was handled well. . . . She helped me begin to find myself
again. I hope the process never stops. . . . I'm sure that everyone
doesn't have such a positive experience. There were times, when I
was in counselling, that things seemed agonisingly slow and even
hopeless. It is only from my present vantage point, two and a half
years, nearly three years, from my first visit to the Isis Centre, that
I can see it as the turning-point in my downward spiral.' (77-F-33)

The process of 'finding oneself' in this way is described very vividly by
another young woman, who provided a clear account of the developing
value of the sessions for her:

'I talked to the counsellor. At first, actually, I talked *at* the
counsellor, since I had the idea that the point of the session was
for me to pour out all my problems, and all possible information
about myself, as if feeding a computer. At this stage the counsellor
listened, and asked me questions.

'Then gradually it dawned on me that I was talking to a person,
not merely an instrument for attaining greater mental health. I began
to make some effort to interact more with (her), which I felt a
response to, in kind.

'I think the most valuable part of the series of sessions was the
gradual formation of a relationship, with a stronger than usual
awareness of what was going on (on my part, that is). The awareness was partly due to the fact that the onus of taking initiatives
was on me; thus, when I finally did so, I really noticed what was
happening, since it took some effort for me to make an initiative.
I think it was good counselling technique which brought out to me
the extent to which I was passive and inward-looking, and I think
it was a technique of restraint – the counsellor responded more
than initiating. It was a good way of giving me an inkling of the
extent to which I could and should take responsibility for what
I get out of my life.' (80-F-30)

Another client had been appreciative of the fact that his feelings of
autonomy and responsibility had not been undermined in any way:

'What was obviously valuable to me (particularly because of the
nature of the problem) was that I remained in control of my own
decisions — I was never subjected to influence which I might
later have conceived of as undue. As I had felt that I had been
too easily influenced earlier in my life, this was very important.'
(95-M-47)

Another describes very clearly his having to lay aside some initial
expectations, but then responding vigorously to the challenge to take
the initiative himself.

'I expected her to be more aggressive, somehow — in the way of
direct questioning. But she explained that this was not her way
of doing it. I accepted this — that the whole thing had to come
from me. I had expected something more clinical — but accepted
that maybe it didn't work that way. The whole thing is rather
mysterious to me: she was quite prepared to sit in complete
silence, if that was what I wanted — but this made me talk, or feel
I was wasting the time. She summed up the best way of dealing
with me. . . . I came for a special reason, and I would have been
wasting her time and mine if I hadn't got on with it.' (96-M-49)

Where the client could not find a way forward, in which he might
experience the increasing rewards of successfully taking responsibility,
he sometimes suffered acutely. One man spoke of the frustrations and
difficulties of the experience:

'I always felt there was this ambivalence as to who was calling the
shots.
'There were some very difficult times: we just sat in silence. It
felt a bit like the night before, doing one's homework: what the
hell am I going to talk about tomorrow? . . . I was either too
frightened to say what I wanted to talk about — or I couldn't
identify a way through the wall. . . . The problem was my reluctance
to talk about, or my non-awareness of, important issues. There
didn't seem to be the help I needed to break it down.
'There were certainly times when I was very apprehensive about
the sessions, and the responsibility that seemed to be loaded onto
me to conduct them.
'There was a powerful task imposed to bring in material, like a
little boy doing his homework — else we shall sit in one of those
interminable silences. I wouldn't have been here if I hadn't found it
difficult to talk about things I felt vulnerable about or had buried
so deep I couldn't dig them up for myself. It was a paradox — that
I was required to do the digging by myself.
'Her method was to make it my responsibility — perhaps she
could have shared this in some way, so that I could respond?'
(40-M-37)

If a crucial question for the client is how to find a way of taking increasing responsibility for himself, a crucial question for the counsellor is how to facilitate this process and to empathise accurately with the alarm and pain that can be involved. A dilemma always persists, however, since the difficulty for the client exists not only within the realities of his actual relationship with this particular counsellor, but also at the level of the fantasies that operate in his inner world. The last quotation vividly illustrates how this man, finding himself in a perplexing situation in which he becomes aware of his own neediness, rapidly feels unmanned, and like a little boy, unprepared for his school lesson. The counsellor then, regardless of his real qualities, is easily felt to be persecuting and neglectful. If he too rapidly acts to allay these anxieties and so to obscure this experience, the opportunity to observe the dynamics of the interaction, and its illuminating relation to other parts of the client's life, may be lost. On the other hand, if the experience is felt to be too painful, or is not clarified by interpretation, the client may suffer without increasing his understanding.

I have suggested that the counsellor typically takes a listening and responding role, rather than an initiating one, and this is borne out by the accounts quoted so far. In some instances, however, perhaps where it was perceived that the client needed rather more active help, this was supplied. One client spoke of 'a lot of interaction' in the sessions, and help in focusing on specific issues. In other cases it was notable that the client spoke quite naturally of the work 'we' did, as opposed to describing it as though he had been alone. A very clear example of this feeling of working together is supplied in the following quotation:

'With regard to my sense of no worth, somehow she always ended
the sessions leaving me feeling I had a lot of worth — without
actually verbalising it as such. Her *participation* with me gave me
this feeling, I believe. We really worked together. . . . Being able
to work together upon the problems of me, instead of being
spoken *at* from the other side of a desk, was the most valuable
and valued part of it.' (104-F-48)

Another woman conveys a sense of growing confidence as to how to use the sessions, assisted at first by her counsellor.

'We worked out what would be brought. At first it was not quite
clear. I got much more decisive as to what I would talk about. . . .
Very often it was to do with reassessing something. I would feel
burdened down by a thought or feeling. She would highlight
different aspects of it.
   'The counsellor suggested a different perspective; alternative
views of myself; revaluing. . . . We mainly concentrated on current
events but with reference to childhood.' (89-F-34)

This client said there was much positive feed-back from the counsellor; particularly helpful was the idea that her troubled state was justifiable and could be understood.

Other clients describe situations in which the counsellor took a fairly directive role, and quite considerably determined the course that things took. In all these cases the client described this as acceptable and useful. One man spoke very warmly of the vigour with which his counsellor insisted that they keep to the agreed focus, on his marital problems:

'I felt the counsellor had a very unusual ability to get people to
talk for themselves — and yet was extremely good at keeping them
on the rails. She acted as a critic — a very kind critic on the
whole — and pointed out flaws. . . . She kept it on a very straight
track.' (127-M-38)

Another couple had worked specifically on a sexual problem, both by discussing it in the sessions and trying out suggested techniques at home. A woman who was troubled by acute anxiety symptoms had tried out specific suggestions from the sessions, and reported back the next week:

'The counselling sessions took the form of discussing what had
happened to me — in my life. I was asked to monitor, week by
week, my panic attacks: their strength and how I dealt with them.
And to give a report at the next session.' (56-F-27)

One man had responded particularly to what he heard as the counsellor's challenge to 'stay with all the difficult bits'. He described a very vigorous interaction:

'Quite often I felt that [the counsellor] was being very aggressive.
This was an illuminating reversal of role for me. I felt very secure.
The counsellor took the initiative. Gradually I got confidence to
disclose more — I almost had to learn this. There was a massive
self-deception in my life. The counselling enabled this to change.'
(5-M-25)

It seems that a number of methods evolve within the counselling relationship, in shared efforts to solve the problems of initiative and responsibility. We have seen examples of clients encountering these dilemmas and being helped to go forward and take on the responsibility themselves. We have also seen cases in which the counsellor gave a lot of active help initially, including modelling openness and involvement, and then later allowing the client to take over. In other instances the problem seems, in effect, to have been by-passed, rather than resolved, by the counsellor generally retaining the initiative.

In other cases again, the counsellors were felt to have kept rather rigidly to a formal, passive stance, and their clients were eloquent about the effects produced.

'It didn't come across that he was genuinely with me. I wanted to shake him. There was pressure on me to conform — but no feed-back. I was distressed by not being able to relate to this person as a person; I didn't like the idea that he was playing a role. I wanted genuine feedback. He just seemed so controlled all the time — that's why I wanted to shake him — I wanted reassurance. I was unsure how much support there really was there. It was like looking at a blank sheet of paper. I didn't know if there was sympathy there — I didn't know what kind of response there would be. That lasted right up to the end. I never got to know him — I got very angry with him. I did say something about this: I said to him, he wasn't coming across as a person at all, just a figure. . . . Sometimes I got the impression that he didn't know how to help me — perhaps that was why he was relieved to draw away at the end of the session. Not that he didn't sympathise or want to help — but was unsure what was best for me.' (90-F-37)

This client, in the absence of overtly reassuring responses from the counsellor, seems to project on to him certain convictions she has about herself, in particular her sense of herself as unlikely to arouse sympathy and support, and her fears that she cannot be helped. Some temporary relief may be afforded from these internal enemies if they are attacked in the person of another who at that time seems to represent them. The help that the counsellor may be able to offer is some observation of these processes as they occur in the counselling relationship. The effectiveness of such an effort to help depends then on several factors, including the counsellor's skill, the strength of the alliance he has created with the client as a basis for working towards understanding, and the capacity of the client at that moment to hear what is offered. If the client is at that time finding this very difficult, the counsellor may sometimes modify his response towards a more supportive position, awaiting a time of greater readiness. Alternatively, he may feel it to be potentially more useful to remain consistent in his attempts to think about what is happening and to convey these thoughts. It is clear that much rests, if he chooses the latter course, on the successful *sharing* of these concepts.

In doubt as to how to use the sessions, and feeling considerable pressure to talk, if only to satisfy the counsellor, several clients felt punished or coerced by silence.

'There was a tendency to play the silence game. I felt I was being pressured by silence. As a technique, I don't like it.' (98-M-54)
'There was very much a policy of the counsellor sitting in silence,

waiting for me to initiate things. I found this disappointing. . . .
I used to come away feeling very negative. . . . There was quite a
lot of silence.' (70-F-28)

This client had felt the pressure of this, but was very confused as to
what she ought to be saying. The counsellor had commented that she
was withholding something; the client felt reproved, yet she believed
she had been trying hard. She experienced a mixture of embarrassment
and disappointment:

'If I could have worked out my own problems, I would have done
it on my own. . . . For the majority of the sessions I felt very
disappointed.' (70-F-28)

The regrettable aspect of these interactions is not that the problems
arose, but that the clients felt so alone with them. Their counsellors
became people to be outwitted, or seduced or coerced into some sort
of alliance, but these aims and feelings seem not have been made
explicit or to have become part of the shared work of the client *and*
counsellor. Particularly strong anxieties were provoked by the prospect
of talking about what was going on in the sessions. One person was well
aware that she was avoiding doing so.

'In the sessions we talked, that is, I did much of the talking,
especially at first. . . . I know I was nervous of talking about what
we were doing in the sessions, or what we were hoping to achieve.
I know I held back a lot of emotion I often felt during the sessions:
I was afraid, as well as embarrassed, by the thought of breaking
down.' (87-F-31)

Some feelings arise directly from the counselling relationship and the
interaction of the particular personalities involved; others are transferred
with great force from the client's earlier relationships, and these powerfully restrict the possibilities of the present. The exploration and
illumination of the links involved have a great potential for facilitating
change; their neglect ensures deadlock. One person conveyed the
desperate intensity of her wanting a complete love and reassurance
from her counsellor, and the roots of that longing in the past.

'I talked and wept, and tried to make [the counsellor] say or
express emotion or say things back. Her role? You call it non-
directive, don't you? She became enormously important to me.
I deeply wanted her to say how much she liked me, etc. . . .
I basically wanted her to be my mother.' (106-F-43)

We have seen in this chapter that the issues of initiative and responsibility arise repeatedly in the counselling process. Where these are
successfully resolved, the client experiences a new sense of confidence

and self-direction, which has important implications for his life. Where the problems in these areas are not solved, the outcome may be a serious increase in depression and frustration. It is one of the counsellor's main tasks to enable the client to deal with such problems, and to provide conditions in which this may happen. We go on now to consider some of the factors which clients felt to be powerful in facilitating useful change, and some which seemed to be an active hindrance.

Chapter 7

Helpful and unhelpful factors in the counselling relationship

In the previous chapter, we saw how clients describe some difficulties that are intrinsic to the counselling process. Some found constructive ways of dealing with the problems as they arose, while others seemed to get stuck. One aim of this study was to listen attentively to the clients' accounts, in order to winnow out those factors that seem to facilitate the solution of such problems and to alert ourselves to those which may be a hindrance.

Throughout the interview, in answer to specific questions but also in additional free comments, clients offered their views about many aspects of their experience. Some factors were repeatedly and emphatically put forward as helpful, others were stressed as unhelpful, and there were some about which there were mixed and contrasting opinions. Many issues of central interest to us as counsellors spontaneously emerged, including: aspects of the counsellors' styles of relating, and in particular the balance achieved between objectivity and warmth; clients' feelings about the degree of activity of the counsellor, and the amount and content of his theoretical contributions; the clients' experience of silence in the sessions; contrasting reactions to the practice of offering regular meetings at fixed times, and spontaneous observations about the general atmosphere of the Centre. We look first at the ways in which people described and responded to the personal manner of their counsellors, and their styles of relating. (Both men and women counsellors participated in the study: in quotations from clients the pronoun relevant to the actual counsellor in that instance is used; in the text generally I have followed the convention of using the male form).

The client's view of the counsellor

The counsellor is aiming to achieve a number of complex goals by means of his relationship with his client. One aim is that the client should understand himself better, and, in particular, become aware of the degree to which his own deeply inwoven assumptions about himself and other people affect his daily perceptions and experience. To this end it is important that the counsellor should not be so personally differentiated that his own real characteristics obscure the unconscious processes which are active in the therapeutic relationship. It is the shared observation of such processes, involving the projection of unacknowledged parts of the self, or the transference into the present of images derived from significant relationships in the past, which provides one of the principal learning opportunities for the client.

Such observation, however, is difficult and often disconcerting, and a person could attempt it only in conditions of trust and safety. It involves the sharing of intimate material from the present and the past, and the expression of feelings arising in the sessions, which are only possible if he feels that his counsellor really understands how he feels, and is unequivocally with him. It is important, nevertheless, that the client should also be sure that his counsellor, while empathising with his feelings, is not overwhelmed by them. He looks for a calm and objective contribution from the counsellor, offering ways in which he may think about his feelings, as well as experiencing them.

The counsellor is, therefore, always trying to maintain a balance between the various aspects of his relating to his client: those which are supportive and nurturant, which include punctuality, consistency of manner, complete attentiveness and warmth; those which allow the client's private fantasies and beliefs to come clear; and those which model and stimulate thinking about them. A wide spectrum of possible positions is offered by the many related disciplines: from the relatively impassive, interpretive stance of the psychoanalyst; through the client-centred therapies, with their accent on genuineness, empathy and warmth; to the encounter models, advocating self-disclosure and personal sharing on the part of the therapist. Each counsellor in each setting is necessarily engaged upon evolving his particular balance, appropriate to his own personality and goals, and responsive to those of his clients.

To assist us in thinking about these issues in relation to the work in our particular setting, we turn to our clients' replies to open questions about the nature of the role played by the counsellor in the sessions, and factors in their experience that seemed helpful or otherwise. The replies collected here have the force of the spontaneous emphasis of a significant number of people, who were not guided in their answers by the form or phrasing of specific questions.

There was great consistency of response concerning the counsellor's attitude to the client. Whenever this had conveyed genuine warmth and concern, it was emphasised as being of great importance. Particular adjectives used to describe this attitude included: understanding, helpful, friendly, caring, warm, accepting and supportive. One client used the phrase: 'sympathetic, but much more than that'. Two others emphasised the importance of trust: 'I trusted her implicitly'; 'a most complete trust between us'.

This style of relating seemed to be fundamental to the establishment of the relationship. Then it was important that the counsellor also be felt to be prepared to listen. 'A good listener'; 'experienced at listening to people'; 'prepared to listen'. Aspects of being a good listener included never being shocked, and being non-judgmental, non-critical.

Although warmth and a sympathetic approach were valued, there was also repeated emphasis on the importance of the counsellor being 'detached' from the troubling situation: being 'uninvolved'; 'impartial'; and not known in any other context.

'An outside touchstone, to sort out what seemed to be wrong, what was wrong.' (27-F-23)

Given the security of a trusted relationship, clients were also concerned with the quality of their counsellors' approach to their problems and felt it to be helpful if they were: intelligent; perceptive; honest; objective; sensible; 'able to bring the perspective of much experience'; consistent, in line of thinking and attitude; 'probing, but warm'. Sometimes it was found to be useful if the counsellor could be 'aggressive' or 'blunt' on occasions, and if he could be felt to be 'strong':

'It's a very reassuring feeling when you come up against someone who is strong enough to say something honest to you – and still sit there.' (65-F-31)

One client offered her own summary of what she looks for in a counsellor.

'I need a counsellor who (a) understands me, (b) credits me with intelligence and (c) is impressive enough for me to respect and take notice of.' (54-F-26)

Another emphasised: 'the caring, the listening, the concern'.

Overall, the appreciated characteristics of the counsellor seemed to be those of someone warm, but calm and objective; not imposing on the client, but quite open, and willing to contribute thoughts and ideas; prepared to be honest and to be quite active if necessary. In contrast, counsellors' characteristics that were felt to be unhelpful were all of a kind to lead to and maintain emotional distance between the client and the counsellor, of a disquieting sort. This seemed to arise either if the counsellor was felt to be very passive, or if he seemed to be very strictly controlled. Descriptions of unhelpful characteristics included: passive, 'a bit like a marshmallow or a cushion'; withdrawn; controlled; 'playing a role' as opposed to 'being a person'; 'putting himself in a trained state'; disapproving, critical; 'emotionally remote'. We shall see more clearly some of the effects of these perceived styles of relating if we go on to consider clients' accounts of what was helpful and unhelpful in the way of specific interventions and activities by the counsellors.

Specific contributions made by the counsellors, facilitative and cognitive

We have seen that some counsellor characteristics, as described by the clients, convey particular attitudes to the client himself, while others indicate the qualities of the counsellor's approach to problems and dilemmas. Similarly, some activities by the counsellors may be considered to be primarily facilitative, establishing a background to more active contributions. The overall picture, built up from what clients say that they have found useful, is of quite strenuous, thinking work, rooted in empathy.

The basic contribution made by the counsellor is simply to be 'a person there who's prepared to listen'; 'she let me talk'.

'I just talked about my life so she could learn to understand — and so I could, too. . . . Just that talking mainly does unburden you.'
(53-F-35)
'The fact that I was able to talk to someone, at all, was of great benefit in regard to my problems, when I first came to the Centre.'
(43-M-33)

The atmosphere in which this listening and talking takes place was felt to be crucial. One woman stressed the following important factors:

'that she didn't know me from Adam; didn't judge; wouldn't criticise. I was free to say anything at all — I didn't have to censor or sift.' (108-F-51)
'It was somewhere where I could go to talk about my problems without feeling I was judged in any way.' (56-F-27)
'It helped most knowing that someone accepted (and I believe valued) me for what I really was.' (6-M-25)
'It was easier than talking to friends — one had freedom to expose the whole problem — to make a more rounded decision — to get out of the fog. . . . She was someone to whom I could be open.'
(67-F-28)

Another person said the most helpful thing of all was 'the completely accepting atmosphere'. One woman commented: 'I felt very safe always', and referred to 'a little safe bit of space'.

> 'The main thing was that, no matter what else happened, I knew she would be there on Thursday afternoon. Sometimes that was the only thing that got me through the week.' (77-F-33)

Four women stressed the importance of being in a situation where they could 'drop the coping front'. One was sometimes herself in the position of counsellor and found it 'nice to lay down that role sometimes'. Others spoke of the relief of being able to admit to confusion and weakness:

> 'It's helpful to talk to somebody who, clearly, doesn't expect people to be in complete control of their lives.' (128-F-33)
> 'What a relief it was to be able to say to someone — no, it's *not* all right . . .' (65-F-31)

One aspect, then, of the counsellor's work was felt to be the creation of a supportive, accepting atmosphere, in which the client felt free to be open and spontaneous. Another dimension, about which a great deal of detail was offered, was the counsellor's contribution to the thinking work that could then take place.

One useful role for the counsellor to take was to act 'as a catalyst', to be the agent in contact with whom the client found himself thinking more clearly.

> 'She triggered off thoughts and ideas'. (91-F-34)
> 'She started a new train of thought.' (67-F-28)

More actively, the counsellor is described as offering particular contributions of his own.

> 'Someone who interjected with objective and penetrating things, that one isn't able to see when fighting through the fog of one's own warped ideas.' (88-F-30)
> 'She noticed things we didn't — that was most important.' (129/130-M and F-23/22)
> 'Her comments were perceptive and enlightening, but never very lengthy or inhibiting.' (95-M-47)
> 'The counsellor asked some very acute and penetrating questions. This was marvellous — like flashes of light.' (54-F-26)

Sometimes the counsellor is portrayed as offering possibilities but not in a very insistent way:

> 'She gave me suggestions as to why I felt about certain things, but I felt I was left to draw my own conclusions.' (79-F-32)

In other cases, certain kinds of insistence are described appreciatively:

'She helped me to concentrate on the difficult areas (I would
probably have left some things out).' (66-F-29)
'The counsellor kept at all the difficult bits.' (5-M-25)

In another instance, the client had valued the counsellor's clarity
and determination in keeping to their agreed task: 'She kept it on a
very straight track'. A young man who had found it hard to use the
opportunity to think about the origin and meaning of his anxiety
symptoms, had appreciated some practical suggestions made by his
counsellor, and, particularly, that she encouraged him to: 'stop avoiding
things that made me feel bad, instead of doing them and trying to
face it'.

The counsellor's help was also valued in what may be simply
described as 'sorting things out'. We have seen that a number of people
said they came to the Isis Centre in a state of despairing confusion:
correspondingly, several people identified the help as being to do with
'making some order from the jumble'.

'Many things seemed much straighter, after a few talks.' (52-F-33)
'She always seemed to be able to pick out what was important in
what I was saying.' (54-F-26)
'She did do some ordering in the sense of suggesting priorities
among the problems.' (128-F-33)

Several people stressed the usefulness of being helped to see their
problems 'in a new light'.

'The most helpful parts were where the counsellor threw a
different light on the situations − showed me another way of
seeing some things.' (107-F-48)

One young woman spoke of: 'a window of sanity on a world that was
in a mess' (27-F-23).

'She would highlight different aspects − suggest a different
perspective.' (89-F-34)
'She could often show me a different way of looking at things.'
(56-F-27)

One particular new way of looking at experiences that the counsellor
could contribute was to explore the links between them, and the
patterns that they made. One client commented on the way the counsellor drew attention to 'underlying themes'; another said: 'Things I was
conscious of but hadn't related − all came together'.

One woman stressed that the language in which such ideas were
presented was important:

'She had a particular insight about not using jargon − using
ordinary, straightforward, real language'. (89-F-34)

Some emphasis was also laid on the importance of the positive, encouraging comments made by the counsellor:

'I was encouraged an awful lot – by positive feed-back from the counsellor.' (89-F-34)
'When I think to myself I'm incompetent I hear [the counsellor] saying I'm not – I think this helps.' (26-F-22)
'I was comforted. But it was rational comfort – not somebody just being nice, but providing a lasting source of comfort.' (27-F-23)
'There was compassion but not spurious sympathy.' (104-F-48)

Another person observed that the positive comments were of such worth because of the atmosphere of honesty that had been established.

'People here do not say things like that just to reassure you' (78-F-35).

Another part played by the counsellor that was felt to be valuable was that of encouraging the client to become independent of him. A man who had come for marital sessions with his wife, commented:

'Throughout I had the impression that she was encouraging [my wife] and me to be independent of her – providing us with tools and techniques for us to use. This was very helpful.' (127-M-38)

These clients have been describing some aspects of the counsellor's manner and role which were felt to be helpful. If we turn now to consider some of the difficulties that clients encountered, in terms of the ways in which their counsellors behaved and the demands they were felt to make, we find a variety of problems.

Difficulties experienced by clients

One source of disappointment, mentioned by four clients, was the absence of advice. Several people said they had approached the Centre in the hope of obtaining explicit guidance on specific problems; on finding that this was not offered, some had responded quite positively to working in a different way, while others felt disappointed and frustrated.

'I had hoped for more advice – I was floundering from one choice to another.' (78-F-35)
'I was looking for solutions – but found they were meant to be inside me. I was disappointed.' (97-M-43)
'It becomes frustrating. We've spread it all out, now what next?' (108-F-51)
'To a certain extent, I knew I wanted something I couldn't have, i.e. someone to tell me the answers. I knew it was pointless asking – but I was aware of this all the time.' (55-F-26)

This client described her mixed feelings on this point:

> 'I respected this about the counsellor: she acknowledged that
> there could be no simple answer. There was no pretence that these
> problems were solvable with a pill, or a piece of advice.' (55-F-26)

She contrasted this approach with that of doctors she had consulted; she said she respected it — but still found it hard to bear.

These clients had regretted the absence of advice about their problems; others, as we have already seen, felt the need of more guidance as to how to use the sessions themselves.

> 'I sometimes felt she let me ramble on too much — irrelevant stuff.
> I think it's better on a question and answer basis. It might have
> been better to be *made* to work.' (88-F-30)
> 'He let me ramble on in any direction.' (97-M-43)
> 'I became preoccupied with what I should or shouldn't be doing
> at the Centre. The counsellor would not be drawn into giving me
> advice, on the grounds that I felt many people were giving me
> advice in one form or another, which I resented and which made me
> feel weak and vacillating. Although my counsellor's approach made
> me feel angry, it was justifiable in a sense.' (43-M-33)

These clients convey strong wishes to be guided, led and advised. Some of them also, however, touch upon the resentment that may be aroused by such help, and the danger that the recipient may feel only more hesitant and more doubtful of his own resources. They highlight one of the constant concerns for the counsellor, who tries to balance sensitivity to the client's dependent needs and longings, with respect for his capacity to reach his own decisions about his life. Where these considerations are not successfully clarified, there is risk of the client experiencing fruitless bewilderment and anger, and a chilling sense of still being very much alone with his difficulties.

Several people had wished that their counsellors would play a more active part in the sessions, and some again felt mixed about this.

> 'Sometimes I felt the counsellor should have been more active,
> asked more penetrating questions, revealed more opinions about
> my feelings or actions. But basically just listening to me talk
> enabled me to sort things out from within, perhaps more slowly
> than if she had been less passive.' (39-M-32)
> 'Sometimes I wished she would offer more herself in the way of
> appraisal. But maybe that would not have been helpful in the
> long run.' (2-M-20)
> 'Sometimes I wished she took a more active part.' (1-M-21)
> 'I think she was being what is technically called non-directive.
> I just felt sometimes I needed a push or a lead.' (40-M-37)

'The lady was very calm and very impassive — sometimes I liked that, and other times I did not.' (79-F-32)

Several people described their responses to the anxiety arising from the passive role adopted by the counsellor:

The only negative thing I feared was that the counsellor's policy of silence made me babble nervously. (54-F-26)

Two spoke of bringing material designed to elicit particular responses from the counsellor, rather than really relevant to their own concerns.

'The first few (five or six) sessions were most helpful. Later, I felt I had to think of how to fill in the hour — and think up suitable material (as I thought). I also felt a danger of a 'game-playing' stage possibly being reached, in the sense that I knew then what would make the counsellor react.' (107-F-48)
'I sometimes felt as if I was playing a fruit-machine, groping around for something which the counsellor could make sense of and reward with an interpretation.' (41-M-32)

The quietness of the counsellor seems sometimes to have allowed the client to follow his own train of thought, unimpeded, but in other cases it had become a problem and a distraction in its own right.

'I tended to want to talk to him, because he wouldn't talk to me. He didn't say much.' (97-M-43)

One client felt she produced things just to fill the silence.

'He would only ask what I was thinking. Like at a dinner party, you must earn your keep a bit. . . . I sometimes wondered if I produced reasons, explanations, to order. Were they the real reasons?' (78-F-35)
'He was so wanting me to produce things that I wasn't frightfully productive.' (105-F-47)
'I felt that the counsellor was wanting me to say things, but I didn't know what they were. I would gladly have said them.' (98-M-54)

Another woman expressed mixed feelings about what she called the 'professionalism' of her counsellor. In many respects she had appreciated this, had felt secure and clear, but also sometimes felt bruised by it.

'One day I had been very shocked and upset; after the session I felt very shaky about leaving. I was hurt, then, by the cool, professional manner. I would have liked some warmth then — a cup of tea. I was very angry then — about the situation and with the counsellor. It was difficult to go off again and face it all. The professionalism seemed very unbending.' (89-F-34)

These quotations all illustrate the power of the feelings experienced within the counselling relationship, and the ambivalence inevitably aroused by its limitations and its professional boundaries. Therapeutic work can take place only within the containment of such boundaries, but they also occasion, from time to time, fierce protest.

Clients encountered difficulties arising not only from the nature of their relationships with their counsellors, but also sometimes from the content of the work and its theoretical orientation. Several doubted the usefulness of thinking about childhood experiences, and became angry or impatient if they felt pressed into doing so.

'The counsellor was mainly asking questions, dwelling quite a lot on my past. I had been over this before with other people, and didn't feel it helped me much.' (80-F-30)

Asked if there were aspects of the counselling that she felt were actively unhelpful, one client replied:

'The continual pressure to look at childhood. . . . She was kind of guiding me into looking at childhood, and, although I could see that was relevant, I knew it wasn't the basis of the problem. That's the way I felt at the time.' (69-F-30)

She felt that she and the counsellor were pulling in different directions, but felt helpless to negotiate or insist on a different emphasis.

'I didn't know what was really wrong with me . . . one thing that really bothered me: Freudian psychology. I felt it was being practised on me without that being made explicit.'

Another person expressed considerable contempt and irritation, aroused by some of the interpretations made by his counsellor:

'I found the suggestion that I couldn't make it on occasions (because of snow, for example) explained in terms of "unconscious resistance" funny (ha! ha!), in view of the trouble I had to go to, to get away from work and attend sessions regularly. . . . Being on the receiving end of such inarguable interpretive cliches can be irritating, in so far as they defy logical discussion, even when this is appropriate.' (41-M-32)

One of his objections to the ideas put forward by his counsellor was that they sometimes 'increased his anxiety'.

'Counselling of this kind . . . *increased* my anxiety on occasions, because it dealt with some aspects of my family life that were obviously relevant neither to my current state nor its control.'

Since anxiety had been his presenting problem and he had hoped for concrete advice as to how to eliminate it, he was troubled and angered to find it apparently exacerbated.

Two other people also expressed some misgivings about the negative and difficult feelings that had been stirred up in the course of their counselling experience.

'At the time I didn't know whether there was a great deal of point in focusing on past experiences — I felt I was already pretty self-aware. One thing it did was to bring back some of the old negative feelings I had towards my mother. I'm not sure if this was a good thing or a bad. It frightens me a bit as these feelings come back — I'm frightened of my own aggression. If feelings of aggression had come out during the session, I would have been supported. But was it a good thing or not to rouse them?' (56-F-27)

The other person, also a woman, was still at follow-up troubled by unpleasant memories that had been agitated by discussion. She conveyed that she was still quite troubled by the liveliness of memories she wanted to get rid of. She asserted, as a principle that she supports, that it is useful and beneficial to deal with buried problems, yet, more feelingly, expressed distress at unwanted memories intruding into her mind.

'It's very annoying when you keep remembering something that you don't want to. This hadn't happened before — I had closed my mind.' (55-F-26)

This person seemed to have striven, against the current of the counselling process, to keep her disturbing feelings out of her mind. This effort had become increasingly difficult to sustain. Her response may be contrasted with that of another woman, who felt that the most helpful experience of all was to be encouraged to express her feelings and to feel entitled to them. She had experienced much rejection, in the immediate and far past, and in panic and rage was, in her words, currently 'tearing up relationships' all about her. She spoke of her counsellor conveying these ideas to her:

'Express what you feel and it will get better. Name feelings. You are entitled to feelings of anger and grief. This was the most important thing: entitlement.' (106-F-43)

Several people had felt increasingly despondent because they seemed to make so little progress.

'At first there was a certain amount of relief, but gradually I felt it wasn't doing me any good. This made me feel even more isolated.' (69-F-30)
'I had hoped for more, but realise now there was probably no more that could be done.' (80-F-30)

One woman looked back on the experience with a rather desolate patience:

> 'There's so much they can do, and the rest . . . you have to do on
> your own. You can't expect too much from people. I was
> expecting too much. It was really up to me to be patient. . . .
> Of course, we always expect more than what we get.' (53-F-35)

Overall, it is perhaps true to say that these clients were expressing reservations of two main kinds. One type arose from a sense of distance between client and counsellor that could not be bridged. When the client felt unsure that the counsellor was truly involved and concerned, it seems that communication inevitably broke down. The client either withdrew in anger and disillusionment, or became fruitlessly occupied in efforts to attract the counsellor's attention. Clearly, such a situation may arise from a great number of alternative or contributing causes, originating in fact or fantasy. In many instances it expressed a critical element of the client's problems outside the sessions as well, and was potentially an area for useful exploration. It is also the case, however, that certain counsellor styles were felt to exacerbate or to alleviate this kind of difficulty. Willingness to become involved, but without directing or imposing on the client, appeared to be a facilitating factor, whereas passive inscrutability was felt to be an additional obstacle and irritant.

The second type of difficulty concerned the content of the sessions and the theoretical framework used by the counsellor. Two particular assumptions were called into question: that the past is relevant to the present; and, that one is likely to be able to deal better with disturbing feelings if one dares to look at them directly, than if one expends energy on keeping them out of sight. This assumption is also related to the concept of unconscious motivation, and requires a willingness to suspend one's familiar explanations of one's own and others' behaviour, in order to see them afresh.

These concepts are fundamental to what a counsellor trained in psychodynamic processes can offer, and he works in the belief that they are valuable. It may be, however, that counsellors can too easily assume that such concepts are self-evident, and so neglect to explain the thinking that lies behind them. One girl complained, not simply about the theoretical background that she gathered was involved, but about its not being made explicit. A man conveyed that he was both baffled and bored by his counsellor's unexplained interest in his past:

> 'I was asked to remember odd things from childhood. I did
> remember odd and unrelated things. But they were not remembered
> because they were important. The counsellor attempted to get me
> to interpret what I remembered. She didn't offer any possible
> interpretation.' (98-M-54)

The evidence suggests that some of these stalemate situations might have been resolved if the counsellors had been more willing to explain their thinking, and to accompany their clients more closely in applying these thoughts to their lives.

The structure of the sessions, individually and as a whole: beginnings and endings

We have considered so far factors emphasised by clients as helpful or unhelpful, that arose within the counselling relationship or in the content of the discussions. Another dimension to consider is that of the structure of the sessions. It is our policy to offer fifty-minute sessions, usually at intervals of a week, and for counsellors to be scrupulous about being punctual for the beginning of each session, and firm about the boundary of its ending. This policy has obvious practical advantages for the regulation of the service. It also, as suggested in chapter 2, embodies the twin provision of security, and the expectation that the client will take responsibility for and contain his feelings between sessions. I have put together those comments that occurred throughout the interview, spontaneously or as parts of answers to other questions, which concerned coming and going, the timing of the sessions, and their structure as a whole. It is essential that the counsellor should be sensitively attuned to the client's feelings about these matters and able to explore them with him.

Several people described considerable apprehension about coming at all.

'Coming here is inclined to be rather worrying — frightening in a way.' (96-M-49)
'Initially I was anxious about coming off the street and through the door — a little paranoid about that. There's no way the Isis Centre could make that different. You're bound to be anxious at some point anyway.' (5-M-25)
'I never got over feeling self-conscious about coming — and rather ashamed.' (109-F-54)
'I was extremely nervous about making the first approach — it was such an unknown quantity.' (70-F-28)

The intensity of the feelings that may be involved was emphasised by the client who felt a resurgence of them as she came back into the Centre, for the follow-up interview.

'I felt it was somewhere I could come. Even though I always felt quite sick about coming — even today. It's extraordinary!' (51-F-32)

Leaving the Centre and going back out into the street again could also be difficult to bear:

81

'Coming in here and coming down to rock-bottom — and having
to go out at the end of the hour. Being back in the ordinary
situation — being a loving mum. The world seems to be going on
so smoothly.' (78-F-35)

In general, the counsellors at the Centre are likely to wait quietly at
the beginning of a session, so that the client may himself choose and
develop its opening mood and content. It is well, however, to appreciate
the acuteness of the feelings that may occur in these minutes, for the
beginning of each session was found to have been extremely troubling
to some: 'having to open sessions myself' (65-F-31).

'I always found the opening five minutes an absolute torture.
I didn't want to take the initiative. Rationally I can see the
importance of my having to make the effort. On the other hand,
the excruciating discomfort could have been lessened a bit by
some kind of lead-in. I just felt very exposed, I think.' (90-F-37)

Another person mentioned his feelings about the sessions ending
punctually:

'I was disconcerted to see that sessions ended at n o'clock,
whatever the state of discussion.' (41-M-32)

One woman was adamant that the session *never* felt long enough.

'I was always frustrated by the sense of fifty minutes not being
enough. One had cried and cried, but not said lots of things.'
(106-F-43)

She felt that a professional approach to emotional problems was
intrinsically flawed, and spoke quite bitterly about it.

'You come desperate. They say: right, Thursday fortnight.
You cry and cry — they send you off without even a cup of
tea.'

She felt that it is sometimes actively dangerous,

'to push people out before they have calmed down a bit. . . .
The difficulty of this kind of situation is: how much can
one help people (a) at all? (b) impersonally?'

Some people felt that there were disadvantages in the system of
regular, fixed appointments:

'I dislike meeting, by arrangement, for an arranged period of time,
for an event which is so emotionally charged, and creates such a
dependence. Without implying anything nasty, it puts one in mind
of going to a prostitute.' (6-M-25)
'I feel that I need a friend or someone I can talk to *when I need*

to talk, rather than at a prescribed time once a week or once a fortnight.' (80-F-30)

'I did find it very difficult to discuss my problems at a specific time. My problems were mainly of an emotional nature and, therefore, one week I might be feeling emotionally a little more secure, and therefore less able to pin my mind down to discussing the overwhelming depression I was experiencing on other days. I felt I needed to be able to talk at a time when I was under the worst pressure of my feelings, though I quite appreciate the impossibility of such a facility! But, on the other hand, perhaps having to go out and talk to someone at a specific time did ultimately have a beneficial effect.' (68-F-32)

These comments contrast with those of two men who each were emphatic about the value of the regularity of the sessions. One, when asked to specify helpful aspects of the sessions, replied, 'Their regularity!' He found this provided both discipline and security, but, particularly, the agreed time was a safe time — he no longer need fear that he was losing touch with people. The other man was describing the marital sessions he had had with his wife.

'What was very, very important in the early stages: a sense of someone being available the next Monday to sort out tangles as they arose — who would not only listen sympathetically, but would also analyse and take to pieces our behaviour — help us understand. There were manageable periods of time, so panic couldn't escalate. This was *very* important.' (127-M-38)

A woman described a similar sense of security:

'She would be there every week; something and someone I could count on, in an attempt to provide me a "roof".' (77-F-33)

I have described the counsellor as constantly concerning himself with various kinds of balance in the sessions, as between objectivity and personal warmth, or between nurturance of the needy parts of his client's personality, and high expectations of his capacity to be self-reliant. He seeks, too, to maintain an appropriate balance in the interaction with any particular client between the degree to which he unreservedly follows the client's train of thought, offering only his response to and interpretations of that flow, and the degree to which he actively helps the client choose and focus upon the most important issues. The fact that it is essential to be flexible in this regard is under-lined by the clients' contrasting opinions about the usefulness of a clear structure to each session, as opposed to complete freedom to range widely and go wherever one's thoughts led. One woman spoke appreciatively of 'a good deal of structure in each session — to focus on a specific issue'; and another man was grateful for his counsellor's insistence on concentrating on their agreed task. This same man's wife had had some individual sessions, as well as their conjoint ones, and it is interesting that, although she saw the same counsellor as her husband, the two relationships had· been very different and the wife spoke warmly of quite a different feature:

'The freedom to range so widely helped to restore my confidence. When one is very anxious and under a great strain, one is liable to get indiscriminately anxious. To talk about it helps to keep proportion, and to shed guilt. I had begun to feel responsible for the whole world. . . . I have a feeling that a more focused path might have operated against this.' (128-F-33)

Another woman spoke appreciatively of the freedom to express her own thoughts and feelings:

'To take what I felt was the most acute problem first, but flexibly, so that I was free to bring anything up for discussion. I was invited to be as freely open as I wished to be — to cry, to break down, or anything. . . . I was encouraged to speak as I felt. [My counsellor] seemed to sense that I needed more than anything to be free, to break many years of repression. Had the counsellor been the "brusque" or "clinical" type of personality, I would not have been able to begin. As it was, the relationship was so natural and so positive I had no fears.' (104-F-48)

These feelings resemble those of another person, who felt that she had been repressing her feelings so intensely that she barely experienced them at all.

'My counsellor made it absolutely clear that anything was OK.' (51-F-32)

She emphasised the value of the 'flexibility', the 'non-expectation':

'It revived some feeling in me, because at the stage I came I don't think I had any at all.'

A debate is found, too, about the overall pattern of the sessions, particularly in cases where a limited number of sessions was proposed, and then reviewed and perhaps extended. One man had rapidly responded to the challenge of this:

'There were several groups of sessions offered — so there was always a possibly final date coming up. I think I thought, well, there's no purpose in waffling around. It made it hard — to discuss a problem you've never discussed before — but it was impossible to avoid.
'I was given the impression in a kindly way that long-term

treatment was not offered. This was a good thing: I felt I mustn't waste time, I must get cracking.' (96-M-49)

Others had had very mixed feelings about this structure:

'She would say: we'll try it for three weeks — we'll try it for another three weeks. I was thankful that she would have me for that long.' (109-F-54)

This person had both longed for and feared an offer of open-ended meetings. Another woman described her experience in this way:

'The first couple of sessions, I was afraid that he wouldn't find my problems worth discussing. I dreaded that there'd be only one or two sessions, and then I'd be sent off. I was in panic lest I'd be thrown out abruptly. I couldn't completely relax — I was upset by the series of potential cut-off points.' (90-F-37)

Another person described similar feelings as she spoke of her anger at termination, but her feelings of constraint about expressing that anger

'because the counsellor is nice to see you at all. . . . There is a feeling of being continually on trial — not a sense of firmness about it. And you can't really say that, because of a feeling of being indebted — otherwise you won't be able to come along at all.' (25-F-22)

This woman felt that the constraining sense of indebtedness arose also because she was not paying directly for the counselling, as the Centre is a National Health resource. Her comment on this point contrasted directly with that of another person, who felt she had been able to come only because it was free. This was not because of poverty but because of a bitter conviction:

'I was not worth paying for.' (51-F-32)

One outcome of her counselling was that her self-esteem improved to the point that she felt justified in seeking private therapy. This represented a marked change from what she described as her 'abysmal self-image.'

Another aspect of the sessions about which several people commented concerned the sex and age of the counsellors they saw. One woman had felt uneasy about talking to someone considerably younger than herself:

'I occasionally thought: "You just don't know — so much has happened to me". A young person can't see things in the same way.' (108-F-51)

This woman suggested that it might be useful to have one session and then review, and change counsellors, if it seems appropriate. A couple who came together did, in fact, do that: they first talked to a male counsellor and then, in agreement with him, changed to a female one. They felt they then 'managed much better'. A man who found great difficulty with the female counsellor he saw, wondered: 'might it have been easier with a man?' but felt unsure about this. A woman client who had seen a female counsellor had valued this very much, and emphasised the importance of being able to talk to another *woman* about her problems. She contrasted this situation with that with her mother: 'I can't talk to her about anything!' Another woman had been disconcerted at first, both by the fact of her counsellor being a man and by his being younger than herself. She soon took this up, though, as an opportunity and a challenge, and found it useful to hear a 'man's point of view'. She said she liked his making 'astute comments' — she enjoyed this about men, and it reminded her of her father.

The nature and atmosphere of the place as a whole; the role of the receptionist

A number of people made some general comments about the atmosphere of the Isis Centre as a whole, speaking of their overall experience there as having been 'positive and warm', or of the 'friendliness of the whole place'. Someone else called it 'a good place to come along to'. Another characterised it as a place where you are 'allowed to be a person'. She felt it was very important that it clearly was not a hospital, and was concerned with people and not 'patients'. She felt the place and the attitude it embodied mattered very much. Her feelings were echoed by another person:

'There was no sense of rush: there was a very quick end to any sense of apology felt for needing help. I was given my place as a person in need, and this was new to me.' (104-F-48)

She contrasted this with former treatment she had received, when she had felt she was 'treated "in parts" . . . but never known as a whole person'.

Some specific factors that were appreciated were: the promptness of the initial appointment, and the punctuality of subsequent ones; an atmosphere of 'quietness, discretion, efficiency'; the respect for confidentiality.

'There are no forms to fill in; no changing of counsellors, so that an essential relationship can build up between counsellor and client — this alone provides one of its greatest aids, constancy of person, place and purpose. The actual simple system of appointments and rooms gives the increasingly rare commodity of privacy and quiet welcome. . . .' (104-F-48)

Several people specifically mentioned the role of the receptionist and her contribution to their experience as a whole. One woman had appreciated and felt encouraged by her 'little smile as you come in', and a man said, 'I was received and greeted in the most discreet fashion.' Another referred to the 'very reassuring receptionist' and she was described as 'someone who made you feel like a person, a human being'. 'She always made me feel welcome — in person or on the phone.'

Three people offered some ideas about the role of such places as the Isis Centre in relation to people's feelings about emotional problems generally:

'One thing I'm very grateful for: that places like this exist. I feel they have an important role to play in dispelling fears of mental ill health.' (69-F-30)

'In view of the stigma still attached by many to the idea of psychiatric treatment, and the often rushed and cold atmosphere of the G.P.'s surgery, a lot of people with emotional problems are put off seeking help. The one to one contact with my counsellor was, for me, the most satisfactory way of receiving help. I think there ought to be a centre of this type in most large towns and cities.' (79-F-32)

'I appreciated the confidentiality and the open-door policy of the Isis Centre. I also appreciated its attempt to distance itself from the medical/psychiatric context of which I have a healthy distrust. . . . The most attractive aspect of the Isis Centre to me was its normalisation of personal/emotional problems. . . . The idea of a chain of such "street shops" into which people could walk and seek help with life-tasks they are confronted with, would be a major advance in moving from a system which focuses on mental illness, to one concerned with mental health.' (41-M-32)

Chapter 8

Outcome

We have seen now something of the range of experience in which people were involved in the course of counselling. We know too the variety and intensity of the feelings that could be aroused. We turn next to hear what our clients reported as the outcome of these experiences. What consequences for their lives did they have? The question asked was: Have you experienced any changes, good or bad, that you think may have come about because of your counselling experience?

When we considered the problems which clients described as having led them to seek help, and the areas in which they hoped for change, we found a few major categories: intensity of distressing feelings; problems in relationships, both specific and general; difficulty in coping with everyday tasks, at home or at work; and some specific symptoms and physical disorders. These categories occur again when we look at areas in which clients report beneficial changes; in addition, they speak of having acquired new ways of thinking about and understanding themselves and their experiences.

Changes in feelings

A change that one would quite confidently predict after even a brief period of counselling is relief of feelings, simply as a result of their having been shared. The freedom to talk, and perhaps cry, openly, in an accepting atmosphere, is one of the basic provisions of the therapeutic relationship. We do, indeed, find that many people spoke of their depression having been relieved:

'My mood lightened: I started to feel better soon after coming here.' (26-F-22)
'I'm much happier within myself.' (54-F-26)
'I don't feel so low.' (97-M-43)

'I'm much happier than when I started!' (95-M-47)
'Things aren't any easier – they never will be. But I'm not
depressed. Even have some zest for the problems!' (105-F-47)
'There was a tremendous sense of release and relief.' (96-M-49)

One person felt unsure how to separate the effects of counselling
from those of a recent course of acupuncture but did say:

'I'm beginning to feel I'm coming out of a long tunnel, into the
fresh air and sunshine.' (109-F-54)

Another group of people stressed relief of anxiety as an outcome
of their counselling. Two people looked back to particularly anxious
periods in their lives:

'It helped contain the anxiety and distress at the time.' (67-F-28)
'It helped contain the anxiety during my pregnancy.' (56-F-27)

A woman whose presenting problem had been severe anxiety attacks
had had none since her contact with the Centre. She was cautious in
claiming to be 'cured', however, as she felt she had not been very
stressed by circumstances during this period. A man whose initial
problem had been acute anxiety, which was interfering with his effectiveness at work, declared:

'One good change is that I have subsequently decided that I am
not anxious at all!' (41-M-32)

He explained that he meant by this that he no longer feared feelings of
anxiety, but regarded them as a normal response to some stressful
situations. This seemed to have modified the degree of anxiety he
experienced.

One woman commented that her anxiety was now 'less overwhelming – less about superficial things'; she confidently knew that she
would calm down. Another said:

'I don't get into that feeling of total isolation and depression – I
can sort out reasons for feeling low. I generally feel more optimistic;
I can weather the low times better – I expect to come through.'
(90-F-37)

A man said he 'got calmer', and another spoke of the experience as
'immensely helpful and relieving'. One woman said she was no longer in
fear about either her own or her husband's mental state.

A somewhat paradoxical effect of facing one's feelings more
directly, and expressing even those that had seemed so shameful or
distressing, is a reduction in the tendency to dislike and punish oneself.
Many emotional changes that were described were due to changes in
self-esteem, and in feelings about the self. Some quotations will
illustrate how many people felt much more accepting of themselves

than they had before, feeling that they understood themselves more accurately, strengths and weaknesses alike, but were also more tolerant of the whole:

'I am much more tolerant towards myself. I can look round for a less accusing view-point, and find it.' (89-F-34)
'I am not castigating myself so much.' (27-F-23)
'I feel more positive about myself.' (78-F-35)
'I can accept limitations in my character without feeling so distressed about them.' (108-F-51)
'I understand my temperamental weaknesses better — but I feel more accepting of them.' (128-F-33)
'I have come to terms with my own emotions. I'm much more relaxed — less self-conscious.' (5-M-25)

Two young men reported a general change in their personal styles of living and relating:

'I'm more aware, and less intense about things.' (3-M-23)
'It has made me more mellow, more settled (mature?) of judgment, and more content generally.' (2-M-20)

Six people spoke of varying degrees of increase in self-confidence. For example:

'I felt incredibly more confident.' (65-F-31)
'I do feel stronger in myself.' (90-F-37)
'I realised that I am strong enough to go on, come what may.' (78-F-35)

One woman who had been intensely depressed and bewildered at the time of the break up of her marriage wrote a detailed account of the changes in her feelings about herself and their consequences for her life:

'My self-image and self-confidence improved to the point that I was able to choose to return to the States, to the city of my choice (3,000 miles from my family) and begin life again. I was able to seek help here when I knew I needed it. I was able to get a job and have done well. In fact, I have grown from a person who was unable to handle the most routine tasks at times, into a confident, cheerful person. . . . I have adjusted reasonably well to living alone, and enjoy being responsible for myself. I have rediscovered excitement and adventure in life. The foundation upon which this is all built is my very positive experience with the Isis Centre. I have made many friends, but still have a little trouble with close relationships. That will come in time!' (77-F-33)

In an earlier chapter I contended that the experience of having some of one's needs met, within clear and safe boundaries, lays the foundation of security and self-esteem from which greater self-reliance springs. This does seem to be borne out by the reported experience of several of our clients who described a greater sense of independence and purposefulness in their lives:

'I achieved what I'd hoped for in terms of grasping my own independence.' (89-F-34)

'I'm very much more on the way to deciding what I want out of life, and more in control of where I'm going.' (65-F-31)

'I have begun to find out how I want to live.' (1-M-21)

'I'm more prepared to take decisions about matters which I know may have emotional repercussions. I have been more prepared to act in ways which risked losing the approval of people I know.' (95-M-47)

Two women in their early thirties had felt relieved of an anxious urgency to be married:

'I'm no longer afraid of being on my own. I no longer think blindly: I *must* be married.' (88-F-30)

'I'm less eager to be married at all costs.' (65-F-31)

Two other women felt freed of an obstructive weight of self-pity:

'I suffer from arthritis, but I understand better how to cope with the condition, and do not feel so sorry for myself as I have done in the past.' (52-F-33)

'I got rethinking properly — off this awful self-pity thing — it got me back rethinking.' (105-F-47)

Another wrote at length about her sense of worth and wholeness being restored, and of a great increase in personal confidence.

'The counselling I received involved the whole of me, so that I could accept the negative parts of me I shunned, and integrate them with the positive side.' (104-F-48)

One effect of these changes in self-esteem and self-awareness was that many clients found themselves now to be more expressive of their needs and feelings to others:

'I found it was OK to say what I wanted.' (65-F-31)

'I stick up for myself.' (27-F-23)

'I'm slightly less apologetic about seeking help.' (89-F-34)

'I can be physical. I'm much more open about my feelings.' (5-M-25)

'I'm less timid about explaining how I feel and why.' (78-F-35)

'At least now I tend to get angry rather than upset. (My counselling experience seems to have released an inhibition over losing my temper!)' (54-F-26)

'The counselling gave me the opportunity to start talking to
people, and not to bottle everything up continually.' (68-F-32)

Changes in relationships

We have seen that some clients felt changes in mood, and in their
feelings about themselves, and that they also found themselves relating
differently to others. Many described beneficial changes in their feelings
about and relationships with other people. Some did this in a general
way:

'Relationships are now much better.' (52-F-33)
'I am much more able to cope with relationships.' (128-F-33)
'I did become slightly more outgoing after the sessions.' (68-F-32)
'The self knowledge I acquired makes it much easier to have many
friends and makes each relationship more rewarding.' (2-M-20)

Sometimes perceptions of and feelings towards other people had
changed:

'People seem less alarming.' (26-F-22)
'I feel more positive towards people.' (78-F-35)

One person said she had used what she had learned about herself in this
way:

'I now consciously correct for a tendency to read other people as
feeling negative towards me.' (90-F-37)

Sometimes a change in behaviour had elicited a rewarding response:

'I am more open with friends, and find them warmer in response.'
(78-F-35)
'I entered a very good phase as far as my relationships with others
were concerned. I got on well with, and felt happy with a larger
number of people. I felt ensconced in a group which I liked and
which liked me.' (24-F-21)

Greater openness with other people was repeatedly reported:

'I don't mind talking to people about myself — but I can choose.
I can be much more open to most people. I seem to have changed
in so many ways and life and relationships seem to have so many
possibilities.' (5-M-25)
'Becoming more open — more willing to talk to other people.
And also more sympathetic, so others talk to me. This has really
changed the feel of my life, over the past year — a fairly strong,
general effect.' (1-M-21)

This was not the only person who reported greater attentiveness to
and sympathy with other people:

'I think I may have become a better listener to other people.'
(95-M-47)
'It's opened my mind a lot: people who commit crimes go to
prison. . . . I can imagine how frightened they would get.'
(53-F-35)

One person measured the progress she was making by the fact of others approaching her:

'About six weeks ago, I began to feel better. Two people
spontaneously came and talked to me. Somebody wanted me.'
(109-F-54)

One woman illustrated the fact that these changes in one's style of relating are only gradually and sometimes painfully achieved. As her deadened feelings began to revive within the security of the counselling relationship, she at first felt increasingly vulnerable.

'It became in a way more difficult to accept any warm response
from other people. I could accept it from [the counsellor] here –
it was a job; much more, but a job. Having loosened those feelings,
I felt much more vulnerable with other people. This is not healed,
but it is healing. More openness gradually becomes more tolerable.'
(51-F-32)

These people have been describing changes in relationships in general; others reported outcome in terms of various degrees of improvement in specific relationships that had been troubling. One said she was getting on better with her family, and particularly with her mother; there were still difficulties between herself and her father (66-F-29). Seven people spoke of changes in their marriages. e.g.:

'I think I'm more understanding of [my husband's] behaviour.'
(78-F-35)
'Some easing of communication with my husband.' (105-F-47)
'My marriage, which had been on the point of breaking up, now
feels secure – I have more insight into the relationship with my
husband.' (128-F-33)
'There is some improvement in the relationship with my wife –
though it's still far from |perfect. . . . One important result: I
certainly recognised errors of behaviour and attitudes, and felt
I had some means of redressing them, which I didn't have before.
I don't always use the techniques, but they're always there.
Mistakes are recoverable – long moods, etc., don't necessarily
have to continue to no purpose.' (127-M-38)

A woman who had been feeling murderous towards her husband said she still felt exasperated with him, but not so desperate. A couple who came for sessions together reported steady improvement in their sexual relationship, and felt they were also able to talk, and to understand each other better. Two women had acquired new boyfriends and felt happy about these relationships: one was still continuing, the other had finished but it had been a good experience:

> 'I fell in love with someone who also fell in love with me, and we developed a very close relationship, which lasted for six months or so.' (24-F-21)

One person reported a change in her view of relationships in general, and the development of a particular new one.

> 'I learnt that it would be more beneficial to me if I put more passion into relationships than into my work, because I had to acknowledge that I wanted very much to love as well as be loved. A relationship which started during the sessions and which I had inner qualms about — qualms which I wouldn't admit to easily — has continued unbroken since, and has become the basis of a new "me" almost! . . . I think many things did resolve themselves in the end because I did try to act on the things discussed in the counselling sessions. I know that I hate "giving in" as a person, but I did not spoil relationships from that point on, as I had done previously.' (87-F-31)

One woman reported eased relationships with her children; another, with her daughter. A man saw his relationship with his children in a new light:

> 'My eyes were opened to the fact that the children need me, whoever or whatever I am. Better a flawed father than none at all. That is something that I've applied.' (40-M-37)

Changes in ability to cope and work

Another area in which people reported problems, and in which they also speak of beneficial changes having taken place, is that of coping with everyday activities and specific tasks. Some mentioned an increased ability to cope in general. For example:

> 'I feel a lot more able to cope.' (88-F-30)
> 'I am definitely able to conduct many of my activities more efficiently now than before I visited the Isis Centre.' (3-M-23)
> 'I am much more active now than I was before the counselling experience.' (42-M-26)

Two people had had to summon up courage to leave Oxford and embark on new jobs. They felt that they had been helped to accomplish this.

'My counselling experience led me to tackle the move from Oxford and my new job in a positive way.' (54-F-26)
'It is possible that, without encouragement and support, I would not have left Oxford and taken a job.' (42-M-26)

A student who had been unable to work effectively, for emotional reasons, said:

'I now have all my intuitive faculties returned to me. . . .' (2-M-20)

Another student spoke of her experience in this way:

'I became less obsessed with the inadequacy of my work, and also it improved somewhat in quality. . . . I have grown up a good deal since my counselling sessions and I believe that is at least in part *because* of them. I feel able to handle my problems now — counselling gave me an approach to use in doing so.' (24-F-21)

Physical changes

A few people mentioned some physical changes, when considering the outcome of the experience of counselling.

'I am better physically (but I have had some lapses).' (89-F-34)
'My physical symptoms disappeared quite soon after the start of counselling.' (128-F-33)
'My physical health has been very good, especially in the past year: I no longer feel dizzy or "headachy", or produce other symptoms which could be considered psychosomatic.' (87-F-31)

One man reported a reduction in tension, and in the stomach-aches, associated with anxiety, from which he had suffered. Another man also spoke of reduced tension and fewer anxiety symptoms:

'I'm more in control of myself now, nervewise.' (7-M-23)

He was, however, still relying on a small amount of medication each day. Two women reported that they had given up the tablets they had been taking, a goal they had particularly wanted to achieve. Only a few people spontaneously mentioned, as part of their answer to the question about outcome, any change in their use of medication. Further information, derived from answers to other questions, about this, and also about changes in the use of other resources, before and after counselling, is reported in the final chapter.

New ways of thinking

Although one might expect that a person would experience some relief of feelings, and would find himself better able to cope with everyday matters, as a result of a supportive relationship, the longer-term security of these changes is likely to depend on the degree to which the client has evolved or incorporated new ways of thinking about his experience, his feelings, himself and others. Among our clients' accounts there were many reports of fresh ways of thinking and greater self-understanding:

> 'I think I understand myself better than I have ever done.' (52-F-33)
> 'I think I learned quite a lot about myself, which has affected how I feel and how I behave (changed for the better, I think).' (6-M-25)
> 'I feel I know myself better.' (3-M-23)
> 'I had very much more insight into relationships − and felt I understood myself better.' (128-F-33)
> 'Having broken through many barriers and shells which I had built up from childhood against everyone, including myself, I discovered many things, many causes for idiosyncratic reactions. This self-knowledge then became knowledge (or at least half-knowledge) of all my relationships.' (2-M-20)
> 'It is difficult to judge, but I think I have a little more insight now.' (110-F-41)
> 'I have some insight into my problems.' (89-F-34)

People described new ways of thinking, sometimes tentatively and generally:

> 'I have thought in a different way' (91-F-34);

and sometimes emphatically and specifically:

> 'I was encouraged to stand and think what I want, rather than be led by foolishness' (88-F-30)

One person said she had been 'led on to more reading' and 'a much deeper understanding of mental ill health'.

Several people said they now thought about themselves differently, particularly emphasising an ability to be more objective than before:

> 'I feel I have a more objective opinion of myself and can analyse myself more clearly than before.' (42-M-26)

One man had talked about learning 'a technique of objective self-appraisal':

> 'For all I know, counselling, because it was an outlet to the rest of the world from which I felt cut off generally, may have been the one thing which kept me this side of madness, where there is no objectivity at all.' (2-M-20)

Another person spoke of a new habit of observing himself more carefully and trying to understand his own motives:

'If I am defensive I am aware of it and can wonder why.' (5-M-25)

Thinking more objectively had meant for another person being relieved of a feeling of inevitable guilt:

'Realising that blame didn't automatically belong to myself – thinking about responsibility more objectively.' (65-F-31)

This same person had come in, in acute distress, at a time of crisis in her life. Looking back, she felt she had had:

'An opportunity to learn something from a recent, painful experience, rather than just suffer it.'

This sense of having received support at a critical time, which enabled him not only to bear the pain of the experience, but also to learn from it, was similarly expressed by another client.

'I feel that I have successfully adjusted to being single again. I am quite satisfied with my present life style, and I have learned to make friends more easily than before. Some day I would like to be married to or at least be living with a woman again. [My counselling experience] filled a desperate need to have someone to talk to while the upheaval of my marriage break-up was going on, and while I was adjusting to a new life and trying to learn from the experience.' (39-M-32)

Ability to seek further help

One last kind of outcome, that was reported by four clients, was that they went on from counselling at the Isis Centre to another form of help, and were glad they had taken this step. One person had gone on into analysis, and described her counselling as 'a sort of foundation stone' for doing so:

'It made me feel more relaxed about the possibility of having it (analysis). It took out the fear, the embarrassment of it. It also made me want to talk about the problems in a more outward fashion, to bounce my ideas off someone else. It made it possible to talk about things I'd not thought of talking about before.' (25-F-22)

Another person had joined an analytic group, and felt he was continuing there work he had begun in counselling:

'It gets you started. You know what you have got to do, even if you can't do it. . . .' (4-M-23)

Another had gone into private therapy, and said of her counselling:

> 'It helped to initiate an on-going process. It gave me the courage
> to seek elsewhere for help, which I never would have done. . . .
> What had been begun was too important, it *must* be continued.
> (51-F-32)

The fourth person, who came for counselling to help her contain her anxiety during her pregnancy, went on later to behavioural treatment for her problems, after her baby was born, and was glad to have done so.

These were not the only people in the study sample who did go on into other forms of therapy after the termination of counselling, but they are the only ones who spontaneously mentioned this in response to the question about the outcome of the counselling. Information derived from other questions on this subject is included in the final chapter.

Negative effects

So far I have considered the kinds of change, reported by clients, that they thought to be beneficial. They were invited, however, to report any changes, good or bad, that they considered to be an outcome of their counselling experience. Four people mentioned specific negative effects: in one case this was felt to be the only outcome, in the other instances the problems arising were accompanied by some helpful changes.

In the first case the client had felt there was very little communication between himself and his counsellor, and, asked how he felt at the end of his contact with her, he said, 'A sad answer: indifferent.' He felt that nothing had changed for him at all, unless a minimal increase in frustration and depression.

> 'Perhaps, in a very tiny way, it was one more option that led to
> nothing. But, really, I have given it very little thought since.'
> (98-M-54)

Another man expressed much gratitude for the help he had received, but felt somewhat bewildered by an unexpected aspect of the outcome. He had come to disclose and discuss a very worrying sexual problem that he had kept secret for many years. As he grew to trust his counsellor and found he could be open with her, he experienced intense relief – to the extent that 'the original problem no longer exists'. Now, however, six months later, he found himself feeling extremely depressed, and very defenceless in that he could no longer account for his feelings in terms of his original anxieties.

> 'I was able to think to myself afterwards – about the fantasies
> I had brought out into the open: was that all it was? There was
> immediate relief – but it has left some sort of confusion. Almost

as if there are some questions not quite answered. I don't even
know what the questions are. . . . Perhaps I expected too much
perhaps I expected all would be well if this one overbearing problem were solved.' (96-M-49)

This person's experience shows how a symptom or a specific anxiety
may function defensively as an explanation for a wider range of mental
pain than truly belongs to it. The loss of the symptom, and hence a
more direct confrontation with other, more diffuse sources of distress,
entails, after the initial relief, considerable bewilderment and disappointment. The self has then to evolve new methods of dealing with
those problems in living against which the symptom had hitherto
provided some shelter.

Two women described a different kind of negative effect, which
they each experienced. This has already been touched on in terms of
problems that may arise in the course of counselling. The difficulty
involved the resurfacing of unpleasant memories that they had thought
they had dealt with and buried. One of these women had sought help,
during her pregnancy, for the panic states and agoraphobia from which
she suffered. The counselling was circumscribed in time by the
pregnancy, and was undertaken with a view to the client seeking
behavioural treatment, after her baby was born. Although the counselling was primarily supportive in nature, it had led to some linking back
to earlier experiences, and in particular to the client's relationship with
her mother:

'One thing it did was bring back some of the old negative feelings
I had towards my mother. I'm not sure if this was a good thing or
a bad. It frightens me a bit as these feelings come back – I'm
frightened of my own aggression.' (56-F-27)

The counselling did come to an end just before the baby was born, and,
later, as planned, the client sought behavioural treatment for her
problems. This had helped her considerably and, looking back over
the whole experience, she said she did not regret the course things had
taken. There was, nevertheless, some sense of unfinished business.

This was the case, also, for the other person who felt troubled by
memories and feelings that had been brought into consciousness again
in the course of her counselling. She had sought help with difficulties
in relation to her sick father, in the present time, and had found herself
exploring the history of this relationship. This had caused problems,
which she had thought she had solved, to resurface, but, it seems, they
had been inadequately buried again without being resolved. At follow-
up, she said that, as she drove to the Centre today, she again felt
troubled by a vivid, insistent memory that she would rather forget. In
each of these three cases it seems clear that there was further work to

be done. In many cases a counsellor, aware that a client may need to resume counselling later, when he feels ready, will, at termination, stress that this is indeed a possibility. Some clients return to take up this opportunity; comments made by some in the follow-up study suggest that others are, or become, doubtful of their entitlement, and unsure whether it is really open to them to do so. It is important that the counsellor take care, as far as he is able, that this possibility, when appropriate, is not only offered but also heard.

It is important to recognise that the effects of counselling can be powerful, and not necessarily always positive. Particular dangers seem to be those of disappointment and despair, and of lingering disturbance where problems have been revealed but only partially resolved. We must also remember that thirteen people did not reply to our letters requesting their participation in the follow-up study, and four people declined to do so. Although we know nothing of their reasons, it is possible that we might have learned from their accounts something more about neutral outcomes or negative effects of counselling.

Chapter 9

The study sample as a whole: the younger men and women

So far we have examined the material provided by the 52 people who wrote, or came back, to the Isis Centre to tell us about their experiences there. We have learnt something of their problems, and their expectations about possible help, and we have heard how they described the various aspects of their counselling experience and its outcome. We have seen the difficulties that can arise, and the kinds of discouragement and disappointment that sometimes occur.

It is important now to set these comments and descriptions in the context of what happened to *all* the people who came to the Centre during that same period of time. We can draw for this purpose on the written observations made by the counsellors about their interactions with those who came only briefly, and with those whom we were unable to follow up.

One hundred and forty-four people came to the Isis Centre for counselling during the time of the study. They included young men and women who were just leaving home and starting their careers; people with families, trying to cope with the mixed demands of their marriages, their children and their jobs; and older men and women, approaching retirement and trying to solve the dilemmas of the later stages of their lives. In trying to consider their experiences, it soon became clear that meaningful comparisons and observations could only be made within groups which were based on some similarity of problem and life-stage. If we could discover some natural grouping, and observe the experiences of people within each group, we might also be able to learn to predict more accurately whether particular kinds of experience are likely to be beneficial to particular sorts of people.

One simple division to make was to look at the experiences of men and women separately. Annual figures show that, on average, 40 per cent of the Centre's clients are men and 60 per cent are women. The proportion in the study sample was 37 per cent men to 63 per cent women. The somewhat higher representation of women was due to the fact that there was a higher proportion of women (28 per cent men, 72 per cent women) among the established, longer-term clients who were included in the study sample, in addition to those who presented as new clients during the relevant period.

Another natural dimension to consider was that of age, in the belief that some problems that regularly arise are usefully considered as maturational difficulties. These occur as people try to negotiate the transition from one phase of their lives to the next. A certain kinship seemed to be discernible within three groups of clients: those whose ages clustered roughly around twenty, around thirty, and beyond forty. For practical purposes, specific lines have to be drawn and the division used was: clients of twenty-five years or less; those between twenty-six and thirty-nine; and those of forty or more. The full age-range of people in the study was seventeen to sixty-three.

One group that required separate consideration consisted of those clients who presented as couples, with specifically marital problems, and in whose cases the work focused clearly on these. In some cases people came on their own to consider problems within their marriages. In some other instances marital difficulties were among the client's problems but did not become the central concern of the counselling work. Such situations are considered alongside the problems of other members of the same age-group. Where, however, the marital relationship was both offered by a couple as their main problem and became the focus of the work, it seemed most meaningful to observe and compare these cases as a group. Seventeen per cent of the men in the study and 10 per cent of the women were included in this category.

For the remaining clients, combining the divisions by sex and age immediately revealed an interesting pattern. We found that the highest proportion of men was in the youngest group. Their numbers reduced progressively in the older groups. This pattern was in contrast with that presented by the women, for whom the largest number were in their late twenties and thirties, and the next largest were beyond forty. Table 9.1 shows the distribution of men and women in the groups to be considered.

TABLE 9.1 Distribution of clients by sex and age (marital problems to be considered separately)

	Age			Marital problems
	25 or under	26–39	40+	
Men	43%	23%	17%	17%
Women	17%	48%	25%	10%

Comparison of this pattern with those revealed by annual figures shows that the study sample is representative of the Isis Centre client population as a whole in this respect.

The contrasting distribution of men and women clients in the different age-groups suggests that the cultural implications of each stage of life are different for each sex, and that they involve differing degrees of stress. On the other hand, we may be observing contrasting patterns of help-seeking from men and women of different ages, rather than contrasting patterns in the occurrence of problems. Another possibility is that there are more sources of help available elsewhere for groups who are under-represented here, as, for example, adolescent girls and young women, than there are for the equivalent young men.

One purpose of considering what happened to people in each of these groups when they came to the Isis Centre was to extend our thinking about the balance of factors in the distressing circumstances of any particular individual. It may be said that there are three basic aspects to any person's problems: personal, maturational and situational. By the personal factors I mean the unique collection of experiences, assumptions, ideas, hopes, feelings and aims that constitute a particular individual. They are derived from his unique history, and understanding of them is based on exploration and observation of his past and current experiences, and of his plans, hopes and fears about the future.

The personal factors are essentially individual. Nevertheless, we all also share in some common experiences, associated with growing up and growing old. The maturational aspects of a person's problems are those associated with the particular stage in life he has reached, the developmental tasks he has accomplished and those that are ahead of him. Jung was insistent that problems have very different meanings at different points in our lives, and that serious attention should be paid to this fact.

> As a rule, the life of a young person is characterised by a general unfolding and a striving toward concrete ends; his neurosis, if he develops one, can be traced to his hesitation or his shrinking back from this necessity. But the life of an older person is marked by a contraction of forces, by the affirmation of what has been achieved, and the curtailment of further growth. His neurosis comes mainly from his clinging to a youthful attitude which is now out of season. Just as the youthful neurotic is afraid of life, so the older one shrinks back from death. (Jung, 1933)

An appreciation of the point a person has reached in this widening, then stabilising, then contracting prospect provides an essential perspective in which to view his difficulties.

The third aspect of a person's problems I have described as situational. By this I mean the external circumstances of his life, both in terms of its physical setting and of social and family relationships. This aspect also includes the impact of specific life-events, particularly recent ones. It may be that sometimes a person's life has been disrupted less by the effects of a slow accumulation of inadequate defensive measures and distorted perceptions, than by a sudden blow. We have seen in our clients' accounts the decisive effects of experiences of loss or change in bringing them for help, and factors such as these have been the subject of much recent study (e.g. Parkes, 1971).

It is clear that all of these factors, the personal, the maturational and the situational, will be found as different aspects of the problems of any person, and all must be taken into account. The relative emphasis, however, is likely to vary and may also be associated with the factors of sex and life-stage that we are exploring. If this emphasis is accurately perceived, it provides an important guide-line in the design of an experience in the counselling sessions that is likely to be useful to the client. One might hypothesise, for example, that people presenting with problems deriving from situational stress, recent in origin, or from difficulties in accomplishing the next developmental step, may benefit from relatively brief interventions, that will naturally tend to focus on these areas. The counsellor allies himself with strong natural forces which are already tending towards recovery or maturation. If the relevant life-tasks are accurately perceived and clarified, help is likely to be effective, and this constitutes, to a large extent, the preventive aspects of the work. Appropriate help, available at the time of situational or developmental stress, may prevent the person from resorting to maladaptive strategies that are likely to underlie further disorder later. People, on the other hand, who present with difficulties of character and personality that have been laid down over many years may need a longer contact or, indeed, be difficult to help at all. The healing agents, also, are more likely to lie in the pervasive and not entirely conscious effects of the counselling *relationship* and less clearly in the cognitive work that is done. The outcome in such cases is also likely to be less clear-cut and to involve more ambivalent feelings.

We turn now to consider the people in each group, and to see whether their shared characteristics shed any light on their individual experiences. I have included a brief outline of each case, drawn where possible from the client's description of what happened. These outlines are necessarily minimal, and show more about the themes of each age-group than about the dynamics of each case. Reference numbers used elsewhere in the text can be related to these tables of case outlines.

We begin by looking at the experiences of the younger men (Table 9.2). The length of this first table of cases serves to emphasise again the high proportion of male clients in this age-group (43 per cent of all the men). It also reveals, however, the rather large number of young men who approach the Centre but stay for only one or two sessions.

TABLE 9.2 Young men: twenty-five years and under

Total sample: 144, of whom 53 were men
of these 23 were 25 years or under
i.e. 43 per cent

Average number of sessions: 10   Range: 1–41

Ref. no., age, marital status and occupation	Problems	Number of sessions	Outcome
		(Information from clients' accounts)	
(1) 21 years. Single. Student (undergraduate).	Problems with academic work. Insecurity; isolation; obsessional fears.	17: four sessions – he stopped then, but returned; then time-limited work; vacation; review. Agreed termination.	Marked changes: greater confidence; greater openness with others; reduction in tension, somatic complaints and fears. 'This has really changed the feel of my life over the past year'. (Follow-up interview.)
(2) 20 years. Single. Student (undergraduate).	Depression. Relationship difficulties. Study problems.	26: four evaluation, 12 time-limited work. Extended till he left Oxford.	Increased understanding of himself, improvement in relationships. Improved ability to study. He felt he had learned things that he still found valuable. (Follow-up questionnaire.)
(3) 23 years. Single. Student (postgraduate).	Study problems. Relationship difficulties.	16: open-ended at first – then, after nine sessions, an agreement to terminate at Christmas.	'No vast changes'. But said he felt he knew himself better; was more aware, and less intense about things; more efficient about daily activities. (Follow-up questionnaire.)

TABLE 9.2 – CONTINUED

Ref. no., age, marital status and occupation	Problems	Number of sessions	Outcome
(4) 23 years. Single. Student (postgraduate).	'General dissatisfaction with life'. Relationship problems.	33: open-ended work; then work towards termination prior to his joining a therapy group.	He felt there had been changes 'inside, mentally', but that these had not been translated into outside behaviour or relationships. More self-observant; but not sure about benefits of this. Felt he knew more what he had got to do, even if he couldn't do it . . . (Follow-up interview.)
(5) 25 years. Married – later separated. Local government officer.	Break-up of his marriage. 'Total confusion and conflict'. Other difficult relationships.	14: open-ended. Termination when he felt ready. Last three sessions working towards this.	Very explicit and positive about benefits: more relaxed; less self-conscious; more open. More self-observant. 'I seem to have changed in so many ways, and life and relationships seem to have so many possibilities'. (Follow-up questionnaire.)
(6) 25 years. Separated. Student (postgraduate).	Depression (suicidal). Break-up of his marriage. Study problems.	17: open-ended work. End determined by fact of his leaving Oxford.	'I learned quite a lot about myself.' This led to beneficial changes in feelings and behaviour. Confidence supported in leaving Oxford and taking a job. 'Beneficial – but how much can you do?' (Follow-up questionnaire.)
(7) 23 years. Married. Factory worker.	Nervous tension. Acute anxiety states.	41: referred after some sessions to another member of the team for behaviour therapy. Brief period of counselling with another counsellor – then stopped coming. Returned for further sessions with original counsellor. Mutually agreed termination.	Less nervous. 'I'm far better now than I was when I came'. Has changed to a job he likes, has had no time off work. 'Still take tablets, mind you' (Librium, small amount). 'It was helpful – up to a point'. (Follow-up interview.)

NO FOLLOW UP			(Information from counsellors' accounts)
(8) 20 years. Single. Student (undergraduate).	Relationship with girlfriend.	9: worked till he went abroad.	Not followed up because there was no address available. Counsellor felt satisfied with work done in relation to parents, girlfriend, education plans.
(9) 25 years. Single. Student (postgraduate).	Depression; anxiety in social situations. Inability to concentrate, affecting his work. Social isolation.	23: a group of seven sessions; then a gap of seven months; then a further 16 sessions.	Useful exploration of his feelings of inadequacy, and their effects on particular relationships, and in general. Client became less self-conscious and more decisive. Client agreed to complete a follow-up questionnaire, but in the event, two were sent and neither was returned.
(10) 23 years. Single. Student (undergraduate).	Anxieties about homosexuality. Physical anxiety symptoms, and fears about his health, loneliness.	13: some evaluative sessions, then work tapering off until time of his leaving the country.	Some reduction in fears about his physical health. Contacted for follow-up at time he was due to return to England, but no reply.
(11) 25 years. Married. Computer programmer.	Problems in relationship with wife.	4 sessions: three with his wife and one alone. Open to him to return if he wished but he did not. (His wife continued in individual counselling.)	Not followed up, since he came only reluctantly and at his wife's insistence.

TABLE 9.2 – CONTINUED

Ref. no, age, marital status and occupation	Problems	Number of sessions	Outcome
2–3 sessions			
(12) 20 years. Single. Student (polytechnic).	Depression; isolation; study difficulties; drinking problem.	2: mutually agreed at second session.	Student had contacted his GP. Had also got in touch with the counsellor at the Polytechnic and arranged to see her twice a week. Feeling more confident and supported.
(13) twenties. Single. Works in bookshop.	Depression; difficulties in concentrating; withdrawing from other people. Career dilemma.	2: further appointments offered after Christmas if he wished. He did not renew contact.	Some disappointment that counsellor did not resolve career decision for him. Maybe he experienced some relief through talking.
(14) 22 years. Single. Local government clerk.	Work difficulties. Problems in relationships.	2: four evaluative sessions were arranged, but he dropped out, without word.	No apparent change.
(15) 23 years. Single. Works in hospital stores.	Employment problems.	2: he cancelled three further appointments; made another but did not come; made another but did not keep it.	Client was very passive, and demanding advice.

Single sessions

(16) twenties. Single. Student (undergraduate).	Finding out about the Isis Centre with a view to his girlfriend coming.	1: mutually agreed.	He was seeking information and clarification. It seemed to have been a satisfactory consultation.
(17) 19 years. Single. Student (undergraduate).	Intensely unhappy and isolated — in his first term. He was afraid he was going mad.	1: a provisional second appointment was made but it was agreed that he would see his GP, who referred him to psychiatric hospital and his appointment was cancelled.	Helped to take some steps towards getting help.
(18) twenties. Single. Student (postgraduate).	Anxiety about a friend — seeking advice.	1: a second appointment offered and accepted tentatively. Client later phoned to cancel.	Some clarification of responsibility?
(19) twenties. Single. Unemployed (undergraduate drop-out).	He needed some-where to live. Relationship difficulties.	1: client came late and left early. Invited to return next week but not expected. He did not come.	Little contact made. He seemed very disturbed — possibly under influence of drugs.
(20) 25 years. Single. Student (postgraduate).	Relationship with his father — and with his girlfriend.	1: a second appointment was made but he did not come.	Distressed, frightened client. No change.

TABLE 9.2 – CONTINUED

Ref. no., age, marital status and occupation	Problems	Number of sessions	Outcome
(21) twenties. Single. Student (polytechnic).	Relationship with parents. Isolated and bored at college.	1: a second appointment made but he did not come.	Subsequently admitted to psychiatric hospital.
(22) 19 years. Single. Unemployed (school to 16, failed A Levels at C.F.E.).	Depression. Failures in work, education and relationships.	1: a second appointment was made but he did not come. Some doubt about where he would be staying.	No change.
(23) 18 years. Single. Unemployed (school to 16 years).	Acute self-consciousness. Health and employment problems.	1: mutually agreed.	Client had hoped for hypnosis. Somewhat disappointed by not being offered a cure.

A brief survey of some of the facts about this group shows that the majority of its members were single (sixteen of the twenty-three), and highly educated (eighteen of the twenty-three had completed or were engaged in study at the University or the Polytechnic). Their ages ranged from eighteen to twenty-five. They typically complained of depression, tension and anxiety. Their problems often took the form of isolation, and difficulty in making relationships. They also found it hard to concentrate on studying, and were anxious because their work was suffering. More than a third said that they had never had any kind of formal help before, and as a group they had a very low rate of hospital contact for psychiatric consultation or treatment (four of the twenty-three). As we proceed we shall see how this compares with rates for other groups.

A general sketch cannot do justice to the individuals in the group but there do seem to be some salient, shared features. They were characteristically clever, withdrawn young men. They felt extremely confused, uncertain, and painfully muddled, yet they were shut in on themselves and usually presented a rather cool, stern front. They wanted to relate to others, and intellectually succeeded in part in doing so, but inside they felt helpless, hopeless and afraid, and they tended to retreat from opportunities of friendship. Three of them had made rather early marriages which had already been abandoned, or were in difficulties; more typically, they had failed to make intimate relationships and were perplexed as to how to do so. In many respects they seemed to exemplify the conflict between the need for intimacy and the retreat into isolation that Erikson (1950) identifies as the major dilemma at this stage in the life-cycle. George Vaillant, in his study of men at progressive stages in their lives, emphasised the same finding. Those

> who work exclusively with young adult (especially graduate
> student) populations discover that, regardless of diagnosis,
> difficulties surrounding intimacy are the dominant motifs of their
> patients' complaints. The emotional disorders that . . . afflict young
> adults . . . all reflect anguish about or protest against failures at
> intimacy. (Vaillant, 1977)

It seems meaningful to regard the problems of these young men as being, in large part, maturational in nature. The tasks that they are inevitably involved in are those of late adolescence and early adulthood. They are concerned with their sexual and their work roles. They must establish their identities, and negotiate their separation from home and their entry into the adult world. Danial Levinson has been concerned with clarifying the various phases of the individual life-structure, and describes the tasks of this phase as follows:

111

The first task is to start moving out of the pre-adult world: to question the nature of that world and one's place in it; to modify or terminate existing relationships with important persons, groups and institutions; to reappraise and modify the self that had formed in it. Various kinds of separation, ending and transformation must be made as one completes an entire phase of life. The second task is to make a preliminary step into the adult world: to explore its possibilities, to imagine oneself as a participant in it, to consolidate an initial adult identity, to make and test some preliminary choices for adult living. (Levinson, 1977)

If we consider counselling as a means of offering help with some of these tasks, it seems clear that the difficulties and the potential benefits lie in the same area: that of making a relationship. By this I mean a relationship that not only works as an intelligent dialogue, but which also really touches feelings and allows for their recognition and expression. For many of these young men, their intellects serve an effective defensive purpose, making them fairly easy to talk to but quite difficult to feel with. This system serves to control anxiety but does not permit useful change. Another dimension of safety and closeness has to be added if the more intimate, central needs are to be acknowledged and met.

These difficulties may, perhaps, help to explain the marked contrast between the successful interventions that are described by members of this group, and the large number of single sessions. I do not intend to imply that a single session is inevitably a failure, since many different and useful functions may be performed by a brief, single meeting. It is, however, clear that it is different in nature from a longer contact, and it involves a choice by the client away from rather than towards the counsellor.

A consideration of the kinds of outcome of contacts in this group shows that, where the relationship could be established, quite extensive beneficial changes seem to have occurred. Clients convey a sense of greater internal ease and coherence, and say that they feel markedly more warm and open towards others. With the changes in feeling and relating, the ability to concentrate and study returns (see particularly cases 1, 2 and 5).

Nevertheless, the relationship is hard to make. If it tends to settle at a level of intellectual but not emotional sharing, then the needed changes are understood, but are difficult to translate into feelings, behaviour and relationships (e.g. case 4). If the bond is not firmly established at all, the client leaves. It may, too, be characteristic of people in the younger age-groups that they make this decision very rapidly, so that some possibility, at least, of contact must be experienced even in the first session, if the client is to invest sufficient patience to allow a relationship to grow.

We turn now to consider the women clients in the same age-group (Table 9.3). As we have already noted, there is a markedly smaller proportion of women in this age-group than there was of the men (17 per cent of the women, as opposed to 43 per cent of the men). This may, however, be a sign of their tendency to seek help more readily than their male counterparts, rather than less. They may seek it elsewhere and earlier. There was a considerably greater likelihood of their having received help before, in almost half the cases this being in the form of psychiatric treatment. Forty-seven per cent of this group had had hospital contact in relation to their emotional difficulties, as opposed to 18 per cent of the men of the same age. Only 20 per cent of the women in this group had had no psychological help before of any kind, in contrast with 36 per cent of the equivalent men. It is not clear whether adolescent girls make their emotional needs plainer than boys do and so are offered help more readily, or whether they arouse more anxiety when they are troubled, and meet lower expectations in others that they can contain and deal with their difficulties. Are they more threatening, more appealing, or both? Whether or not these are partial explanations, fewer young women than young men come to the Isis Centre, and fewer of them are quite new to psychological help.

Like the young men, they were likely to be single, and in higher education or further training of some sort. They were more expressive of their unhappy feelings and were more explicit about their nature: they included depression, fearfulness, rage, loneliness, anger and anxiety. They associated their difficulties much more directly with their parents and with the problems of leaving home than did the corresponding group of young men. Five of these girls did feel extremely isolated and lonely, but more characteristically they were unhappy and insecure *within* a muddle of relationships, rather than withdrawn and on their own. As with the young men, their emotional turmoil manifested itself in study and work problems, and in making and sustaining relationships generally.

If we consider their pattern of attendance at the Isis Centre, we see that there were relatively fewer very brief contacts in this group than in the corresponding male group. It seems that the young women had less difficulty, as a rule, in starting to make relationships with their counsellors. They also, however, tended to feel less committed when they did so. Even if they settled to work, their average number of sessions was lower than it was for the young men. For those who came four times or more, the average number of sessions for the young women was fifteen, whereas for the young men it was twenty-one. In four of the cases that did establish themselves the client abruptly stopped coming, without explanation. This did not occur at all among the equivalent men. The young women were also more difficult to follow up. Indeed, they are one of the only two groups in which the

TABLE 9.3 Young women: twenty-five years and under

Total sample: 144	91 women of these, 15 were 25 years or under i.e. 17%		
Average number of sessions: 10		Range 1–26	
Ref. no., age, marital status and occupation	Problems	Number of sessions	Outcome
		(Information from clients' accounts)	
(24) 21 years. Single. Student (undergraduate).	Insecurity – affecting study and relationships. 'A sense of over-dependence on my parents'. Depression. Fearfulness.	19: open-ended work; terminated by client's decision.	Very positive about her experience. Reports improvement in relationships, general and specific, and in work. More confident in approaching new problems. (Follow-up questionnaire.)
(25) 22 years. Single. Student (undergraduate).	Emotional problems, adversely affect-ing her studies.	18: evaluation + two terms work. Terminated by client just before exams.	'A sort of foundation stone for going on into analysis'. 'Very helpful'. (Follow-up interview.)
(26) 22 years. Single. Unemployed (undergraduate drop-out).	'Very, very depressed'. Isolated and withdrawn.	22: open-ended work; finished when client felt ready to do so — mutually agreed.	Feels better and finds people less alarming. A little more self-confident but still very vulnerable. Close to tears at follow-up. (Follow-up interview.) (Later, resumed her university course.)

114

| (27) 23 years. Married (had dropped out but later returned to complete her course). | Murderous rage with husband — and suicidal thoughts. Problems in relation to parents, work, home. | 26: evaluation + open-ended work. Termination mutually agreed. | 'I'm more right with myself'. Problems remaining but feels less desperate. There are still marital problems but not so acute. Still problems in relation to her mother. She feels a bit more confident — 'not castigating myself so much; sticking up for myself'. Spoke warmly of her experience, although only limited changes were achieved. (Follow-up interview.) |

No follow-up

(Information from counsellors' accounts)

(28) 19 years. Single. Cleaner (pre-university).	Depressed. Pregnant, away from her own country. Lonely and unhappy.	5: she cancelled her next appointment, saying she did not want to make any more.	Counsellor felt doubtful as to usefulness of the sessions. A follow-up request letter was sent but later returned — she had gone away and left no forwarding address.
(29) 25 years. Single. Unemployed.	Bouts of depression. Unemployment. Feels angry and distrustful.	4: in six weeks — cancelled two. She phoned to cancel next appointment, and did not make another.	Counsellor advised against follow-up. Client had belatedly revealed that she was currently seeing a psychiatrist.
(30) 25 years. Single. Student (undergraduate).	Problems in relationships with parents, with fiancé, and generally.	17: five evaluative sessions, then 12 sessions agreed, determined in advance by date of leaving country.	Counsellor reported that client felt more positively about herself, and felt her own needs and wishes to be valid. Improved relationship with fiancé. She felt less tense and depressed. Enjoyed her work and achieved good results and a good job afterwards. She agreed to complete a follow-up questionnaire but, in the event, two were sent to her and neither was returned.

TABLE 9.3 – CONTINUED

Ref. no., age, marital status and occupation	Problems	Number of sessions	Outcome
(31) 23 years. Single. Unemployed.	Depression; social isolation; low self-esteem. Employment.	11: four evaluative sessions: then a further 12 agreed. After seven it was mutually felt that she needed more support and she was referred to a day hospital.	Possibly some small gains in confidence, enabling her to consider group work at the day hospital. (No reply to either of the two follow-up request letters.)
(32) 20 years. Married. Student (undergraduate).	Sexual anxieties; depression; relationship with parents.	16: work towards her going abroad.	Counsellor advised against follow-up.
2–3 sessions			
(33) 23 years. Married. Secretary.	'In a state over whether or not to leave husband.'	2: cancelled the next session.	It was planned that she should come with her husband for the third session but she phoned to cancel this – saying the problem was resolved.
(34) 17 years. Single. Starting A level course at C.F.E.	Anxious and confused: afraid of madness. Extreme problems with parents. Study problems.	3: of an agreed four.	Cancelled the review session, saying, 'I haven't the patience.'

116

Single sessions

(35) 21 years. Single. Student (postgraduate).	Fear of breaking down; being over-conscientious and unable to relax.	1: she was only in Oxford for a few days.	Counsellor felt the session may have been helpful. Client may look for a counselling agency where she is studying.
(36) 17 years Single. Student on secretarial course.	Difficulties in relationship with mother.	1: cancelled the next session.	Client phoned to cancel her second appointment, saying she had 'sorted herself out'.
(37) 23 years. Single. Student (postgraduate).	Study difficulties; social isolation.	1: cancelled the next session.	No apparent change achieved.
(38) 25 years. Single. Does odd jobs.	Isolation.	1: mutually agreed.	She was seeking some information which was supplied.

117

number of cases that were eligible for follow-up but could not be reached exceeded eligible cases that were followed up successfully.

The outcome of these cases is also more ambiguous. There are only two clear reports of positive change in several areas, and only one of these is derived from the client's account at follow-up (cases 24 and 30). There are some accounts of more specific help (e.g. 25), or more precarious and mixed effects (e.g. 26 and 27), but there are also several rather doubtful ones.

The overall impression is that this group has a different style from that of the male group of the same age. The young women tend to be more expressive, more impetuous, more impatient. One could say that their defensive style tends to be hysterical, whereas the men adopt more schizoid patterns of defence. The women tend to be overwhelmed by feeling while the men strive to repress it. Clearly, the influence of some cultural stereotypes can be seen at work here.

The young women also seemed to have and to take up more opportunities for acting out. They tended to dilute the counselling relationship with others outside, perhaps setting them up in opposition rather than using them to illuminate one another (e.g. psychiatrist or parent *versus* counsellor). It was easier to make superficial relationships with the young women than with the young men, but it was harder to establish work with them. Perhaps one girl summed this up when she exclaimed: 'I haven't the patience!'

If this sketch of two contrasting styles of adaptation is based on real differences, applicable to individual cases and commonly occurring at this point in the life-cycle, it might offer a guideline to the tenor of the necessary work. In the one case this would be to balance thought with feeling, that is, to assist the expression of feeling so that the person experiences himself emotionally as well as intellectually; and in the other case to balance feeling with thought, so that the person can understand, reflect on and regulate an otherwise unruly emotional life.

Chapter 10

Men and women: late twenties and thirties

We move on now to consider the experiences in counselling of the next age group. This includes men and women in their late twenties and thirties. If we look at the sample as a whole, this involved 30 per cent of all the men and 51 per cent of the women. If we reserve for separate study those who presented as couples and worked on specifically marital problems, we have in this group 23 per cent of the men and 48 per cent of the women.

In his study of the features of each stage of adult life, Levinson draws attention to the tasks and dilemmas which characterise each phase. He sees a necessary tension for a person in his twenties between the need to explore possibilities and keep alternatives open, and the need to create a stable life-structure and make commitments, both to particular people and in his working life. He detects a transitional period around the age of thirty, when the provisional, exploratory quality of life is ending and choices start to feel irrevocable and seem to close other possibilities more decisively.

> A truly developmental crisis occurs when a man is having difficulty with the developmental tasks of this period; he finds his present life structure is intolerable, yet seems unable to form a better one. In a severe crisis he experiences a threat to life itself, the danger of chaos and dissolution, the loss of hope for the future. (Levinson, 1977)

The reader may recall the voice of one of our clients, who has already been quoted: 'I experienced a sort of general collapse of self-confidence. . . . I was looking in myself for something firm to cling to, and finding nothing at all; a great, gaping well. . . . I was completely at sea, and didn't see much point in anything' (40-M-37).

Distress at this stage typically appears as protracted hesitation, uncertainty and dissipation of energy. The individual feels helplessly

119

indecisive and lacking in confidence. If the crisis is resolved successfully, important new choices are made or old courses reaffirmed, to which some commitment has already been made. A person's equilibrium then and in the future depends on his ability to settle to chosen tasks and committed relationships, and to direct his energies in a coherent and constructive way.

Table 10.1 gives a brief outline of how each of the men in this age-group fared in counselling. There were in this group six professional men, who had all completed university education; four in manual occupations; and two who were unemployed. Three were single, one of these cohabiting; seven were married and two had been married and were now separated from their wives. Four of the men had children. Five of the seven married men reported severe difficulties in the relationships with their wives.

The prevailing feelings expressed by this group were of anxiety, loss of self-confidence and insecurity. They worried about their work, their marriages, money and sexual problems. In some cases their difficulties resembled those of the younger group of men: intense anxiety in social situations, difficulty in making relationships, loneliness and self-doubt. This resemblance suggests a maturational emphasis in these cases, as thought they were still battling with developmental steps that should have been taken earlier.

Two men were acutely anxious about their work. They had achieved highly at the beginning of their careers, but were now finding it hard to sustain and develop their initial successes.

Five others found that their personal anxieties and difficulties were manifested in and exacerbated by problems in relation to their wives. Two men were suffering from the impact of the recent breakdown of their marriages, events which had placed an intolerable strain on personalities which were already diffident and uncertain in many ways.

Of this group of twelve men, only three had had no help previously for their problems. Some had relied on their family doctors for consultation or medication; two had been in psychotherapy before; six had had psychiatric treatment, in two cases as in-patients.

There is a marked contrast between their pattern of attendance at the Isis Centre and that of the younger men. In the latter case, we saw a rather clear division between those who settled to constructive work and those who came only briefly. In this older group, we see that no one came just once, and nine of the twelve came four or more times. In general they agreed to an orderly structure of work, and no one dropped out abruptly without explanation or agreement.

Nevertheless, in all but perhaps two cases the outcome seems to be tentative and uncertain. The complete accounts of their experiences often convey considerable frustration and disappointment in spite of an overt willingness to comply and to persevere. In general these tended to

TABLE 10.1 Men: twenty-six to thirty-nine years

Total sample: 144, of whom 53 were men
of these, 12 were between the ages of 26 and 39
(excluding those who came with their wives for marital therapy)
i.e. 23%

Average number of sessions: 25   Range 2–123

Ref. no., age, marital status, and occupation	Problems	Number of sessions	Outcome
		(Information from clients' accounts)	
(39) 32 years. Separated. Research scientist.	Problems arising during and after break-up of his marriage. Lack of confidence in establishing and maintaining personal relationships.	30: weekly at first, later at intervals of a fortnight and, finally, a month.	'I feel I have successfully adjusted to being single again. I am quite satisfied with my present life style and I have learned to make friends more easily than before. . . . It filled a desperate need.' (Follow-up questionnaire.)
(40) 37 years. Separated (children of 8 and 6). Writer.	Pain of marriage breaking up. Collapse of self-confidence in all areas: relationships and work. Loss of sense of own identity.	24 sessions: open-ended work for about 18 sessions; then the counsellor suggested work towards termination.	No improvement in regard to main problems – except they have been articulated and identified. A bit less uneasy about his relationship with his children. Still very empty and depressed. (Follow-up interview.)

TABLE 10.1 – CONTINUED

Ref. no., age, marital status and occupation	Problems	Number of sessions	Outcome
(41) 32 years. Married. Lecturer.	Acute anxiety – particularly affecting his work.	17: five evaluative sessions. Then agreed to meet for 12 more sessions.	He no longer considers himself to be anxious, and can cope with things better. He feels that his symptoms have been relieved but is doubtful about attributing this to the counselling. (Follow-up questionnaire.)
(42) 26 years. Married. Postgraduate in further professional training.	Social relationships. Financial problems.	7 + 2: rather intermittent. Client wrote to cancel further sessions.	A little more active; a little more objective about himself. 'Ultimately frustrating as the problem wasn't solved'. (Follow-up questionnaire.)
(43) 33 years. Married (2 children). Self-employed – later unemployed.	Marital difficulties; suicidal impulses; sexual anxieties; 'feelings of inferiority and rage'.	123: weekly sessions. Terminated by mutual agreement.	'In the long term, my problems seem much as they were, and my ability to cope with them not much better. I suppose I have a clearer idea of what the problems are'. (Follow-up questionnaire.)

No follow-up

		(Information from counsellors' accounts)
(44) 39 years. Single. Part-time handyman.	Wanting to understand himself more – having recently had treatment for a drink problem.	13: three evaluative – then an agreement to meet for ten further sessions. Then referred to a therapy group.	Increased understanding of himself. Counsellor felt the sessions were vigorous and useful. There was a long delay, though, before the proposed group formed and the client dropped out and could not be contacted. He agreed to come for a follow-up interview but did not attend. Did not reply to next letter.
(45) Thirties. Married (3 children). Computer programmer.	Anxieties about work; and marital problems.	10: four evaluative; four further sessions agreed. Two more added. Counsellor suggested group therapy.	Doubtful if any change took place. There was a long delay before the group and the client dropped out. He did not reply to follow-up letter. (He returned later for further counselling with another counsellor.)
(46) 34 years. Married. Self-employed.	End of homo-sexual affair. Grief, and anxieties about his marriage.	13: five initially – client chose to stop. Returned two months later: a further eight sessions agreed.	Some alleviation of original distress. Perhaps he became a little more accepting of himself.
(47) 32 years. Married. Artist.	Marital problems: crisis in relation-ship with his wife.	56: four individual evaluative sessions; then it was agreed he should join his wife for marital sessions (22 sessions). He continued individually after this for 30 sessions.	Some improvement in communication with wife. Some work in relation to his long-standing personal difficulties. Counsellor advised against follow-up.

123

TABLE 10.1 – CONTINUED

Ref. no., age, marital status, and occupation	Problems	Number of sessions	Outcome
2 or 3 sessions only			
(48) 27 years. Married. (Children of 6 and 5). Nursing assistant.	Restlessness; indecisiveness; marital problems.	2: this was what the client asked for, having previously had a series of sessions with the same counsellor.	Some relief for having discussed his problems with a trusted confidante.
(49) 32 years. Single.	Depression; lack of confidence; insecurity in relationships and at work. Sexual anxieties.	2: four evaluative sessions were agreed, but second and third were cancelled as counsellor was ill. Client came once more but then left Oxford.	Doubtful as to whether any change took place.
(50) 33 years. Single. Unemployed.	Difficulties in making relationships; wanting a girlfriend.	3: Client left after one, turning down offer of further evaluative sessions. Returned after several weeks for two more sessions, then stopped coming without word.	Restless; fearful; seeming to be increasingly fragmented. Possibly he renewed his existing contact with psychiatric hospital.

be rather passive, dependent men, who seemed to be touchy and irritable rather than defiant or rebellious, and who longed for some clear direction and advice. They tended to feel frustrated and further confused by the exploratory, non-directive methods of their counsellors. At follow-up some expressed contempt or disappointment about this, and felt that their fundamental mood had not been changed much.

For men of this style, at this stage in their lives, the danger seems to be that the counselling relationship may be based more on compliance than on attachment, and that the apparent co-operation is accompanied by an undertone of frustration and disappointment. Once again the indication for the counsellor is that priority must be given to the task of enabling a real relationship to grow, as an essential precursor to cognitive work. The particular skill required lies, perhaps, in providing conditions which facilitate the client's experiencing himself as an effective agent, rather than a passive recipient, in the counselling work and, thence, in his life.

Some notable contrasts will be found as we turn now to consider the experience of the women in the same age-group. As we have already observed, this age-group contained the largest number of women clients. Among their problems, three particular kinds recurred sufficiently frequently to suggest that they might be looked at separately. There were twelve women who presented primarily with difficulties in relationships, particularly with men. Ten of these women were single, and two were divorced and had no children. Each of them came in in distress because she had just lost, or was in danger of losing, a boyfriend, and each saw this as part of a pattern. They were all very aware of the cultural implications for a woman of reaching the age of thirty and being unmarried. Each person was feeling some urgency to sort out her working and social roles, her priorities, and the likelihood of her being able to make a settled relationship with a man and to establish a family. This group of women may be said to be battling with the maturational and cultural problems of this period of life.

A further ten women came to the Isis Centre because of difficulties within their marriages. Two were on the point of deciding to separate from their husbands; others were hoping to avoid this outcome, but were perplexed and almost despairing; others again were hesitating between their husbands, and other men.

A third group who shared some common problems consisted of eight women, all of whom had been recently divorced or separated from their husbands. All but one had small children living with them, and they presented with combinations of: the shock and pain of the breakdown of their marriages; the difficulties of bringing up children alone; and anxieties about future relationships. There were, of course, unique personal elements in every case but they shared the emphasis of the pain of their current situations and of recent events.

The remaining fourteen women within this age-group presented with individual, idiosyncratic problems, and the emphasis of the work fell on the personal, rather than the maturational or situational factors. We shall begin by considering this last group (Table 10.2).

All but two women in this group were single, and they were working in a wide range of occupations, many of which had involved further education and training. Three people were still studying. Ages ranged from twenty-six to thirty-six. Their problems were various and idiosyncratic, and usually involved long-standing difficulties of personality and adaptation. I have explicitly separated them from those cases where the emphasis seemed to be on particular maturational or situational factors. By our original hypothesis, one would expect to find here more intransigent difficulties and ambiguous outcomes.

Nevertheless, as in the parallel group of men, there are still some instances of problems which link with those found in the younger groups, e.g. study problems; difficulties concerned with leaving home; anxiety about an ill father; insecurity about work. There are also some examples of phobic states, obsessional preoccupations and uncontrollable anxiety attacks. We also find instances of some of the deepest disturbance and depression of all the clients. The variety and intensity of their individual problems make generalisations difficult.

Like the men in the same age-range, if these women came to the Centre, they tended to settle to work. Only two came once; all of the others came five or more times, and some had very long contacts indeed. As far as previous experience of psychological help was concerned, they were almost equally divided between those who had none (five); those who had been in counselling or therapy before (four); and those with hospital contacts (three as in-patients and two as outpatients).

We find a range of outcomes. One relatively low-key interaction yielded modest but satisfactory results (case 52). Two interventions with postgraduate students seem to have been helpful (54 and 62). Two pieces of work that were focused in terms of subject matter, and contained within an agreed time limit, seem to have been effective within the range of the agreed area of work, but also to have left some unsettled, uneasy feelings of issues that were raised but not resolved (55 and 56).

The longer interactions were typically very emotional and characterised by violently conflicting feelings. The therapeutic relationship was complex and intense, and both process and outcome in each case was particularly hard to assess at termination; even six months later, the clients who agreed to come for follow-up were strongly moved by returning to the Centre and by recalling their experiences there. They were equalled in number by those who had come for considerable periods but were not followed up. Terminations were, in several cases,

TABLE 10.2 Women: twenty-six to thirty-nine years (individual problems)

Total sample: 144, of whom 91 were women of these, 14 were in this group i.e. 15%

Average number of sessions: 38   Range: 1—246

Ref. no., age, marital status and occupation	Problems	Number of sessions	Outcome
			(Information from clients' accounts)
(51) 32 years. Single. Teacher.	Effects of a serious crisis in her life. Desperate feelings creating a problem of 'sheer physical survival'.	29: over a period of eighteen months.	'I found it was worth continuing the struggle to exist'. 'It gave me the courage to seek elsewhere for help which I would never have done'. She went on into private psychotherapy, still continuing at follow-up. (Follow-up interview.)
(52) 33 years. Single. Shop assistant.	Difficulties encountered (emotionally and in physical health) when she left her parents' home, to live independently.	19: four evaluative sessions. Then fortnightly meetings: 12 sessions — end determined by her then feeling more confident and optimistic. Three further sessions a year later as she was leaving Oxford.	Understands herself better. Improvement in relationships generally. Copes better with the physical condition she suffers from, and feels less depressed. (Follow-up questionnaire.)

TABLE 10.2 – CONTINUED

Ref. no., age, marital status and occupation	Problems	Number of sessions	Outcome
(53) 35 years. Single. Skilled manual worker.	Acute attacks of fear and panic – and fear of harming someone.	15: two evaluative – then work 'until Christmas'. Spaced fortnightly towards end.	She is feeling calmer, but rather precariously so. (Follow-up interview.)
(54) 26 years. Single. Student (postgraduate).	Anxiety and depression, related to D.Phil. thesis. 'A general lack of confidence.'	5: came in only just before leaving Oxford.	Overall: 'It was just what I needed'. Much happier – coped with leaving Oxford and new job. Still has doubts about thesis. (Follow-up questionnaire.)
(55) 26 years. Single. Lecturer.	Anxieties about ill father.	16: time-limited work. Evaluation, then agreed 'until Easter'.	Some help with understanding relationship with father. But a worrying agitation of feelings and memories, stirred up but not resolved. (Follow-up interview.)
(56) 27 years. Married. Nurse.	Phobic anxiety, intensified during her pregnancy.	3 + 11: work until baby was born – then a review.	Contained anxiety during pregnancy. Later referred for behavioural treatment. Some negative feelings stirred up but unresolved. (Follow-up interview.)
No follow-up		(information from counsellors' accounts)	
(57) 30 years. Single. Student.	Relationship difficulties, particularly with a woman friend. Persecutory fantasies.	17: five session evaluation; then an agreed 12, but these rather intermittent towards the end.	Uncertain. Anxieties and fantasies seemed to have been contained, but not basically changed. She did successfully complete her course, and later sent an invitation to an exhibition of her work. She declined to participate in the study – giving her having moved away as a reason, but not offering to complete a questionnaire.

(58) 30 years. Single. Librarian.	Unable to cope with work — very low self-esteem.	6: seen as an assessment.	Referred for behavioural treatment to psychiatric hospital. She did not take this up. Went home, overseas. Counsellor saw no evidence of change in her. Not followed up as no address available.
(59) 36 years. Single. Nurse.	Relationship difficulties, particularly with a woman friend. Uncontrollable states of panic, rage, despair. Suicidal impulses.	85: weekly for over two years. Open-ended long-term work. Rather uncertain termination, while she made arrangements for private psychoanalysis.	Some reduction in panic and suicidal wish. Groundwork for choosing analysis. Counsellor advised against follow-up. (Two years later, client called in of her own accord, to let her counsellor know that things are going well for her. She was about to get married.)
(60) 28 years. Single. Unemployed (formerly a teacher).	Intense anxieties; a belief that she is unacceptable to others.	50: four session evaluation. Then open-ended work. Terminated by client, who made arrangements for behavioural treatment.	Counsellor advised against follow-up. Client later returned for further counselling.
(61) 30 years. Single. Teacher.	Fear of madness; severe depression.	246: weekly, or twice a week, over a period of four and a half years.	Not followed up, but hopeful prognosis in counsellor's view.
(62) 29 years. Single. Student (postgraduate).	Insecurity in work and relationships; uncertainties about career.	27: in groups over a period of four years.	Not followed up as not truly terminated. Counsellor is confident about her progress, reported increased confidence and independence, and felt useful work had been done regarding family relationships and career decisions. Increased self-esteem.

TABLE 10.2 – CONTINUED

Ref. no., age, marital status and occupation	Problems	Number of sessions	Outcome
Single sessions			
(63) 29 years. Single. Nanny.	Worrying about continuing need of anti-depressants.	1: mutually agreed. Consultation with counsellor with whom she had previously had a long series of sessions.	Client said it was helpful to clarify her feelings. Counsellor felt this was a useful and appropriate contact. (This client later returned for further work.)
(64) 30 years. Married. Unknown.	Drug addiction.	1: mutually agreed.	Information gathering and exploring alternatives.

complicated and painful to achieve, and in four instances the counsellor advised against renewing contact.

Bearing these examples in mind, we shall now look at the three other groups of women within this age-range, beginning with those who presented primarily with difficulties in relationships with men (Table 10.3).

All but two of the women in this group also were single: the other two were divorced and living alone. With few exceptions, they had high levels of education and of achievement in their jobs. A glance at the column in the table which shows their problems will reveal their similarity. Typically they came in as a result of the distress arising from the latest in a series of troubled or lost relationships with boyfriends. Five were experiencing the pain of a recent parting; six were in difficulties with a current boyfriend and recognised these problems as part of a familiar pattern; several saw themselves as generally finding it hard to make and sustain relationships, particularly with men.

Of these twelve women, five had not sought help of any kind before. (This is the highest proportion in any group.) Only one had had hospital contact, as an in-patient; five had some experience of counselling. The low rate of medical consultation suggests that these women generally did not think of themselves as ill, and had shown an effective level of adaptation until now. Their problems may be regarded as primarily maturational, and their urgency was directly associated with their age. As a group they strikingly resemble the young women discussed in a paper by Shaw (1977), in which she considered the relationship of their problems to the nature of their interaction with their fathers during adolescence.

At the time of their approaching the Centre, these clients were very distressed, some feeling themselves to be in a 'crisis', due to the recent loss of someone they cared for. They were aware of a need for constructive change in themselves, and their active distress offered the energy with which to accomplish this. There was also swift agreement between them and their counsellors as to the nature of the problem.

It will be seen that only one person came once, and another three times. Ten of the twelve came four or more times, and we have follow-up data from six of these.

The potential for positive change, facilitated by counselling, seems to be great for women at this point in their lives, and experiencing this kind of problem. There were some very positive reports at follow-up (e.g. cases 65 and 66) and in one case from the counsellor's account (73). Useful change seems to have occurred in several other cases. In two cases, however (69 and 70), the clients' accounts conveyed acute disappointment and frustration. In each of these cases, the counsellor had taken a rather formal, analytic approach, concentrating on the client's early childhood experiences, without having established an

TABLE 10.3 Women: twenty-six to thirty-nine years (presenting primarily with difficulties in relationships with men)

Total sample: 144, of whom 91 were women
of these, 12 were in this group
i.e. 13 per cent

Average number of sessions: 19   Range: 1–51

Ref. no., age, marital status and occupation	Problems	Number of sessions	Outcome
		(Information from clients' accounts)	
(65) 31 years. Single. Student undergraduate (formerly, nurse).	Crisis of end of relationship with man-friend; feeling abandoned by him.	13: three session evaluation. Agreed to meet and review after summer holiday. Agreed then to meet 'till Christmas' and did so.	Client spoke very positively; reported increased confidence and decisiveness, and a sense of being more in control of her life. Also, less preoccupied by wish to be married at any cost. (Follow-up interview.)
(66) 29 years. Single. Nurse.	Problems in relation to boyfriend, and to family (particularly to father).	25: evaluation; some open-ended work; then work towards joining a therapy group.	Overall impression: 'positive and warm'. Client said she felt much more accepting of family; improved relationship with mother; still problems with father. Anxieties less overwhelming, and less about superficial things. (Still in therapy group.) (Follow-up interview.)
(67) 28 years. Single. Secretary.	Pressure of work and difficulty in relationship with man-friend.	12: two series of sessions, each at a crisis point. Three sessions in first series; nine in second series, three years later. Termination each time as crisis abated and she felt able to cope on her own.	Anxiety and distress were contained and relieved at the time. Some ideas incorporated then still seem useful and relevant. (Follow-up interview.)

(68) 32 years. Single. Supervisor in a shop.	Depression, related to relationship with boyfriend. Problems at work. Anxiety about 'elderly and incapacitated mother'.	4: evaluation followed by suggestion that she join a psychodrama group, which she did.	Client reported that she felt 'slightly more out-going after the sessions'. An opportunity to 'start talking to people and not bottling everything up continually'. Still has some doubts about her 'social abilities'. (Follow-up questionnaire.)
(69) 30 years. Single. Works in publishing.	Depression; loss of boyfriend; difficulty in forming relationships.	10: open-ended at first; then to finish when she joined a therapy group.	Dispelled some fears about 'mental ill-health'. But no impact on the depression. (Dropped out of therapy group almost immediately. Found it 'barbarous'.) (Follow-up interview.)
(70) 28 years. Single. Artist (teaches part-time).	Depression and anxiety dating from death of father and associated with several insecure relationships with men. Loss of interest in work, and creative ability.	15: three session evaluation — then an agreed 12 sessions.	Some short-term relief but still markedly depressed and anxious. (Follow-up interview.)

133

TABLE 10.3 – CONTINUED

Ref. no., age, marital status and occupation	Problems	Number of sessions	Outcome
		(Information from counsellors' accounts)	
No follow-up			
(71) 26 years. Single. Nurse.	Blushing at work; impending separation from boyfriend; difficulty in making lasting relationships with men; strong, conflicting feelings towards parents.	9 sessions: four evaluative sessions; then five more until she left the country.	Blushing much reduced; some insight gained into persisting strength of ties with parents. Not followed up, as no address available abroad. (Letter sent to English address but no reply.)
(72) 34 years. Single. Works in publishing.	Feelings of loneliness and abandonment, following move from another city and away from lover.	45: open-ended; expected to be 'fairly long-term'. Termination finally planned for when she joined a psychodrama group. (She did so, but dropped out almost immediately.)	Client seemed less depressed and no longer suicidal. Difficult, rather confused termination. She refused to participate in the study. Added a bitter note.
(73) 27 years. Single. Student (postgraduate).	Problems in relationships, especially with men – recent loss of boyfriend.	38: four session evaluation, then weekly sessions until client went abroad.	Client reported positive changes in many areas – these comments formed basis of counsellor's account of the outcome; more open and more expressive of both vulnerability and anger; less need to control and keep controlled; useful exploration of her role, and feelings about being a woman. Improvement in academic work. Resumed own writing. She agreed to complete a follow-up questionnaire but in the event two were sent to her (overseas) and neither was returned.

134

(74) 29 years. Single. Unemployed (left school at 15 years).	Employment difficulties. Sexual anxieties. Difficulty in making or sustaining relationships.	51: initial period of about three months. Then work towards her having sufficient confidence to take up opportunity of group work at day centre.	The main aim of the work was to enable her to make the step towards therapy in a group setting, and this was achieved. (No reply to follow-up request letter.)

3 sessions only

(75) 37 years. Divorced. Lecturer.	Debating whether or not to accept a recent proposal of marriage. Career dilemmas.	3: agreed to meet weekly in the three weeks left before going abroad.	Useful clarification of choices and priorities.

1 session only

(76) 29 years. Divorced. Unemployed (graduate).	Problems in relationship with boyfriend; seen as part of a pattern of difficulties in such relationships.	1: counsellor did not offer a second session as client had already made an appointment with Marriage Guidance Council.	Perhaps some clarification of choices.

alliance within the relationship or an agreement to work in this way. It is possible that these clients could have worked more usefully if attention had been paid to the specific characteristics of the current phase of their lives, as a precursor to making explanatory links with the past. These are perhaps examples of situations in which the problem could usefully have been defined and approached as maturational, rather than as arising mainly from individual psychopathology.

The next group of women within this age-group had in common problems within their marriages (Table 10.4). All but two of these married women had one or more children. Some also had jobs outside the home, and two helped their husbands in businesses run from where they lived (a public house, and a farm). The two women who had no children were both working, but one somewhat beneath her training and capacities.

Three people had had no formal help before; three had had hospital treatment, one as an inpatient. Four had received help at some time, from a doctor, a psychologist, a social worker, and the Isis Centre on a previous occasion. Their ages ranged from twenty-six to thirty-eight.

Their kinship with one another lies in the fact that their presenting area of concern was marital stress. In three instances this arose directly between themselves and their husbands; in seven cases it was caused by or reflected in their own or their husbands' infidelity.

They came for relatively brief series of sessions at the Isis Centre, half of them coming four times or less. The person who came only once had already resolved to leave her husband and, although extremely distressed, was anxious not to be dissuaded. Of those who came two or three times only, all seem to have used the time to clarify their thoughts about their situations, without wishing to commit themselves to further work at the Centre. One of these decided to return to the Marriage Guidance Council, where she had already had some sessions. Two other people (cases 78 and 82) felt that they had got as far as they could on their own, and left it that they might return with their husbands, if they would agree. One of these women (78) felt that she was better equipped, after her counselling sessions, with confidence and understanding with which to meet the difficulties of her marriage.

Another person had finally agreed with her husband that they should separate and she felt that the work she had done with her counsellor had restored her confidence, and had enabled her to set out on a new life with some energy and hope (77). Another was less emphatic about the changes achieved (79), and another was polite, but clear that little had changed (80).

The decisive factor in these interactions is the client's motivation, which seems to be a particularly problematic factor within this group. Where the work succeeds, it is perhaps in cases where the client is willing to use her current life situation as a starting point and an urgent

TABLE 10.4 Women: twenty-six to thirty-nine years (presenting primarily with marital difficulties)

Total Sample: 144, of these, 91 were women
of these, 10 were in this group
i.e. 11 per cent

Average number of sessions: 7   Range: 1–22

Ref. no. age, marital status and occupation	Problems	Number of sessions	Outcome
			(Information from clients' accounts)
(77) 33 years. Separated, then divorced. Horticultural work.	Depression; inability to cope with every-day matters; living apart from husband. Very low self-esteem.	22:: five evaluative sessions. Then open-ended work. Three joint sessions with husband. Termination agreed when client felt confident and ready.	Client wrote detailed, positive account. Improved self-image and self-confidence. Has established herself independently, has a home and a job. Completed divorce arrangements. Feels confident and optimistic. (Follow-up questionnaire.)
(78) 35 years. Married (one child, four years; baby expected). Housewife.	Problem of deciding between her marriage and her relationship with another man.	7: open-ended till client decided not to continue unless her husband would agree to come too.	Client had decided to commit herself to her marriage — welcoming coming baby. Feels more positive about self and others. More expressive of needs and feelings. More confident — more understanding. Marriage still is difficult, but not overwhelmingly so. (Follow-up interview.)
(79) 32 years. Married (one child, nine years). Family business.	Depression; marital problems.	9: four evaluative sessions; open-ended work, terminated when client felt confident to do so.	Rather less depressed but still experiencing quite marked mood swings. 'I think I did know myself a little better'. (Follow-up questionnaire.)

TABLE 10.4 – CONTINUED

Ref. no., age, marital status and occupation	Problems	Number of sessions	Outcome
(80) 30 years. Married (two children, 6½ and 3 years). Housewife.	Agoraphobia; depression. Difficulties in relationships with children and husband.	7: fortnightly sessions. Seen as an evaluative series, then recommended to approach day hospital. (She went twice and then stopped).	No improvement in health, agoraphobia or relationships. 'It was not unhelpful, but not directly helpful'. (Follow-up questionnaire.)
No follow up		(Information from counsellors' accounts)	
(81) 28 years. Married (two children, 10 and 5 years). Housewife.	Depression; marital stress (husband's infidelity).	13: open-ended work until client expressed readiness to stop.	Counsellor felt that client had used the opportunity for further maturation, and increased in confidence, realism and independence. (Client said she did not want to participate in the study.)
(82) 32 years. Married (two children, 13 and 6 years). Housewife.	Marital problems; husband's infidelity.	4: four evaluative sessions agreed at outset. Agreement to stop then, unless husband would come too.	Perhaps some clarification of what is possible. Client had hoped for intervention to change husband.

2–3 sessions only

(83) 38 years. Married (two children, 14 and 10 years). Research worker.	Marital stress.	3: evaluative sessions; client decided to return to Marriage Guidance where she already had made contact.	Relief of immediate crisis by verbalising anger against husband.
(84) Thirties. Married (two children, 10 and 8 years). In professional training.	Marital problems. Husband's infidelity.	2: at the second session it was agreed to have one or two more, but the client cancelled these.	She wrote to say that she had been enabled to make a positive move in the difficult situation at home.
(85) Thirties. Married (two children). Farmer's wife.	Marital problems. Living with husband and lover.	2: with interval of one month between them. Cancelled next appointment.	No apparent change, although client said she had been thinking a great deal about her situation.

Single session

(86) 26 years. Married. Local government officer.	Marital crisis: dilemma between husband and another man.	1: she came with her husband at his insistence. Did not want to come again with him, or alone.	No change (her husband continued in individual counselling).

reason for understanding herself better. Where it falters, it seems to be associated with mixed expectations as to what is possible, including the hope that someone else, e.g. one's husband, may be miraculously *made* to change. There are also instances (e.g. 85, 86) where the client experiences the difficulties of her situation, but is nevertheless very reluctant for it to change.

The elements of clarification and negotiation play a large part in these interactions. The counsellor has to devote quite a lot of work to establishing a shared base from which he and the client can proceed. In a considerable number of cases, it appears that there is not really a mutual agreement to use the time for personal exploration and reflection. The outcome in these cases, and the difficulties involved, may be contrasted with those arising in the following group, who shared problems arising from broken marriages and the responsibilities of young families. The experience of finding themselves suddenly on their own again, after some years of marriage, led people to take up the opportunity to reflect on their own contributions to this event with some urgency and energy (Table 10.5).

This is a relatively small group but the consistency of the problems presented justified separate consideration. Ages ranged from thirty to thirty-eight. All but one of the women had children living with them; all but one were engaged in employment or study outside the home.

A feature of their presentation at the Centre was their extreme distress. They spoke of suicidal impulses, loneliness, anger, tension, confusion and despair. They were beset both by the painful feelings associated with the events of their marriages and their breakdown, and by those arising in their current lives, often characterised by loneliness and difficult responsibilities. We have seen the acute loss of confidence experienced by some of the men after the failure of their marriages, and this is shared by these women. They were more likely, however, to be very expressive of their feelings than the men were, and less likely to be passively bowed down by them. The undercurrent in this group was of angry protest rather than subdued discouragement.

Perhaps an indicator of their expressiveness is that only one of these women had had no help for her distress before coming to the Isis Centre. Several had turned for help to their doctors, and three had had psychiatric treatment, as outpatients. At the Isis Centre, none came only once; one came three times and the remainder came eight times or more. There were no extremely long contacts, in contrast with those we have seen in the other groups of women in this age-range.

The problems in this group are the most clearly 'situational' in nature, and seem to support the expectation that moderate interventions in such cases may achieve good results.

There was a high rate of positive outcome and five of the seven people contacted provided follow-up information. Although the

TABLE 10.5 Women: twenty-six to thirty-nine years (with problems arising after divorce or separation)

Total sample: 144, of whom 91 were women
of these, 8 were in this group
i.e. 9 per cent

Average number of sessions: 17   Range: 3–35

Ref. no., age, marital status and occupation	Problems	Number of sessions	Outcome
		(Information from clients' accounts)	
(87) 31 years. Separated and co-habiting. Teacher of English as a foreign language.	Acute distress – suicidal impulses. Isolated and lonely. Uneasy in relationships and insecure in her job. 'The break-up of my marriage and an affair had led to the above crisis'.	27: open-ended work. Termination when client left Oxford.	Client wrote positively about her experience. Different, less negative feelings about herself. Improvements in relationships generally, and with a particular man friend. 'I did not spoil relationships from that point on, as I had done previously.' Good changes in physical health. (Follow-up questionnaire.)
(88) 30 years. Divorced (one child, 6 years).	Financial and emotional problems of being a single parent. Difficulties in relationships with men. Lack of confidence. Anger with self and the world.	11: open-ended work. Mutual agreement to stop, when client felt confident and ready.	Much more able to cope generally. Had made a good relationship with a man. Less afraid of being alone. Greater confidence and independence. (Follow-up interview.)

141

TABLE 10.5 – CONTINUED

Ref. no., age, marital status and occupation	Problems	Number of sessions	Outcome
(89) 34 years. Separated (two children, 11 and 9 years). Housewife.	Marital crisis – husband decided to leave her. 'Physically and emotionally I couldn't cope.' Very low self-esteem.	18: six week evaluation; then agreed to work 'until Christmas'.	More tolerant towards self; less self-accusing. Better physically. More able to accept appropriate help. 'I achieved what I'd hoped in terms of grasping my own independence'. (Follow-up interview.)
(90) 37 years. Separated (one child, 8 years). Teacher.	Depression; tension; confusion and despair. Family problems concerning custody of child. Weary of relying on tranquillisers. Work anxieties.	19: four session evaluation. A further six agreed, then a further nine.	'All the little bits fitting together'. More able to cope. More confident at work. Less despairing. But still using medication to help her control depression and anxiety. (Later returned for further counselling.) (Follow-up interview.)
(91) 34 years. Separated (two children, 8 and 4). Student (formerly nurse).	Marital crisis: her husband left her. Uncontrollable distress.	14: one session – then transferred to another counsellor, when original one was ill. Open-ended work – end determined by counsellor's leaving.	Tentatively: 'I have thought in a different way'. But she had been unable to recover from the original change of counsellor, and from loss experienced at termination. Confirmed in her despair about anyone being able to stay with her. (Later she spontaneously let us know that she is feeling much better, and coping well with family and work.) (Follow-up interview.)

142

(Information from counsellors' accounts)

No follow-up

(92) 38 years, Separated (one child, 12 years). Mature student.

Problems in relationship with man friend.

8: had one of an agreed four. Then cancelled. Later returned – seven more. Agreed number at outset.

Counsellor felt that some useful work was done towards her taking more responsibility for her actions, and understanding jealous feelings more. (Did not reply to follow-up letters.)

(93) 30 years. Separated (one child, 4 years). Student on secretarial course.

Distressed, angry, lonely; frustrated by difficulties of single parent-hood. Problems in relationships with men.

35: four evaluative sessions; a further six agreed; extended as an agreement to meet for a further eight months.

Improved relationship with mother. More self-confidence socially. More coping self-image, and greater interest and confidence in work. Little change in relation to father or feelings about relationships in the past; little change in feelings about sexuality. (No follow-up as she did not reply to either of two request letters.)

3 sessions only

(94) Thirties, Divorced (two children, 16 and 13 years). Research worker.

Depression; social withdrawal. A number of lost relationships.

3 sessions: she failed to keep the fourth of four evaluative sessions.

Counsellor felt that client had avoided the review session – perhaps unable to face up to possibility of separation then.

143

occasion of coming for counselling had been specific and distressing, work in the sessions was by no means confined to a narrow focus. Clients report changes in their attitudes to themselves and to others, and convey a sense of people emerging from crises in their lives in a stronger position than they had held before, being more tolerant, more realistic and more confident. They exemplify Caplan's (1964) concept that a crisis can be an opportunity rather than a catastrophe, if a person uses it to evolve more effective adaptive capacities than he has hitherto employed.

It is important, however, that the potent element of loss in such cases be fully appreciated. It is essential that the relationship is established with the utmost security and care. In the only case in this group which terminated abruptly (94), the counsellor suspected that fear of a possible separation may have prevented the client attending the fourth of four evaluative sessions. It is possible that her fear of rejection prevented her from entering into the negotiation which might well, in fact, have led to further work.

The other case which demonstrates the extreme sensitivity of such feelings at times of loss is that in which there was an unavoidable change of counsellor after the first session (91). Although a new attachment was made, and useful work done, at follow-up the client's feelings were dominated by the despair she had experienced at her apparent abandonment by her original counsellor. It too perfectly echoed and reinforced her powerful feelings at the time. It is possible that observation and discussion of this fact in the follow-up interview may have helped in the healing process. The client took pains later to let us know her better news.

In the following chapter we shall consider the experiences of men and women in the older age-group.

Chapter 11

Men and women beyond forty

The older age-group, of people of forty or more, contained fewer men but about a quarter of all the women. The oldest man in this sample was fifty-four, but the oldest woman was sixty-three.

The common problems and tasks of this period of life can be observed in many areas: in relation to family and friends; associated with work, from mid-career to retirement; and in relation to the self. In Elliot Jacques' words:

> 'The individual has stopped growing up, and has begun to grow old.'

He suggests that the special features of this phase of life derive from the fact that the reality of the approach of one's own personal death is beginning to press into awareness.

> 'The sense of the agedness of parents, coupled with the maturing
> of children into adults, contributes strongly to the sense of ageing –
> the sense that it is one's own turn next to grow old and die.'
> (Jacques, 1965)

He draws attention to the paradox that a sense of being an established adult is accompanied by an awareness that that achievement is dated. 'Death lies beyond'. Successful adaptation depends on the development of what Jacques describes as 'constructive resignation': an ability to accept the shortcomings and the shortness of one's life without being overwhelmed by bitterness and despair.

Erikson (1950) defines the potential strength of this stage of life by his term 'generativity'. In this he includes mature productivity and creativity in one's own fields of work and self-expression, and also the ability to invest hope and care in the achievements and efforts of one's own and others' children. Such generativity matures, in its turn, into a condition of dignity and acceptance which permits a fearless going forward towards death. Where these maturing processes fail or are

145

checked, the individual is at the mercy of 'a pervading sense of stagnation and personal impoverishment'. This mood leads only to impotent protest and despair.

We turn now to look at the particular examples of problems arising during these later years as they were presented by the men in our study (Table 11.1). A glance at the family circumstances of all the men in this group shows the prevalence of experiences of unease or loss. Seven of the nine men were living on their own, five of them having been divorced from their wives and separated from their children. The general level of capacity and achievement was lower than in the younger groups, and problems of unemployment and housing were presented in several cases.

The prevailing feelings were of depression and dissatisfaction. The two married men were disappointed and restless, both at home and at work. The others were oppressed by loneliness: in the words of one, 'feeling redundant and abandoned'.

This group had the highest rate of all for hospital care for their emotional problems. Three had had outpatient treatment and three had been in-patients. The others had sought help before from the Isis Centre, from the Marriage Guidance Council or from the Samaritans. Only one person had never sought help at all.

As can be seen from the table, two men came only once, each apparently being under a misapprehension as to what the Centre could offer. Two came very briefly, one of whom already knew his counsellor well. The remainder came between nine and twenty-four times.

The four men who provided follow-up information exemplify an interesting range of responses to their counselling. One man (case 95) reported significant, beneficial changes. He experienced a revival of hope and purpose, and went on to develop his career in ways he had hoped for but had hitherto hesitated to pursue. He seemed to have sorted out some aspects of his marriage, his work and his personality which could not change and would have to be accepted. In the process, he also clarified some ways in which he *could* make constructive changes.

The second person (case 96) offered a very moving account of his release from sexual anxieties that had tormented him since he was an adolescent. The experience of sharing these, in an atmosphere of compassion and acceptance, had afforded him great pain, followed by intense relief. Nevertheless, some months later, he was grappling with a more insidious problem in the form of pervasive depression. A second layer of distress was now demanding attention. This was composed of the various losses in his life, including and maybe activated by the termination of his sessions with his counsellor to whom he had made a strong attachment.

Another man conveyed quite another mood at follow-up. His

TABLE 11.1 Men: aged forty years and over

Total sample: 144, of whom 53 were men of these, 9 were forty or over i.e. 17 per cent

Average number of sessions: 10   Range: 1—24

Ref. no., age, marital status and occupation	Problems	Number of sessions	Outcome
		(Information from clients' accounts)	
(95) 47 years. Married (three children, 21, 19 and 18 years). Teacher.	Family problems; dissatisfaction with work.	9: open-ended work; ended when client felt ready.	He felt more decisive — and more able to take difficult decisions. 'A better listener' to others. More critically aware of his need for approval and less governed by it. He spoke positively of the experience. (Follow-up questionnaire.)
(96) 49 years. Divorced (one child, 21 years). Business manager (later unemployed).	Tension; depression; sexual anxieties.	23: open-ended work; ended by agreement when client felt he had accomplished his main aim.	'A tremendous sense of release and relief'. Original problem no longer exists. Yet later felt very depressed and found this hard to deal with. Very positive about his relationship with the counsellor. (Follow-up interview.)
(97) 43 years. Married (three children, 17, 16 and 14 years). Lecturer.	Marital and family problems. Dissatisfaction with work. Loneliness.	8 + 16: first series ended when counsellor left. Second series, with another counsellor: open-ended, terminated by mutual agreement.	Some slight amelioration of problems, but achieved by resignation rather than by constructive change. 'The benefits are rather intangible but probably exist'. (Follow-up interview.)

TABLE 11.1 — CONTINUED

Ref. no., age, marital status and occupation	Problems	Number of sessions	Outcome
(98) 54 years. Divorced (two children, 27 and 25 years). Unemployed.	Depression. 'Impotence' — sexually and generally.	16: four evaluative sessions, then two more — then ten agreed and completed.	No change. 'Perhaps, in a very tiny way, it was one more option that led to nothing'. (Follow-up interview.)
No follow up		(Information from counsellors' accounts)	
(99) 40 years. Divorced (children, no details). Unemployed.	Unemployment. Loneliness. Difficulties with authority. Defences based on fantasies.	10: he was already known to the counsellor. These sessions were completed — a further appointment agreed for three months thence. Intermittent contact after that.	Not truly terminated and so not followed up. Some stabilising effect achieved by limited but open-ended contact?
2–3 sessions			
(100) Fifties. Divorced (one child, 12 years). Unemployed.	Unemployment. Living situation unsatisfactory. Poverty.	2: agreed and kept, with a client whom the counsellor had seen previously and knew well.	Relief of feelings — some comfort and reassurance. Information gained on a particular issue.
(101) Forties. Divorced (three children, 12, 9 and 7 years). Technical fitter.	Depression after his divorce. Feeling redundant and abandoned.	3: evaluative sessions agreed. Client chose not to continue beyond this.	Client seemed very passive in the sessions. He did report that he felt less depressed and had taken on a few more activities.

Single sessions

(102) 50 years. Marital status not known. Unemployed.	Physical symptoms. Housing. Practical and emotional worries.	1: mutually agreed – little contact made.	Client disorientated or possibly drunk. Unlikely to be helped at Isis Centre.
(103) Fifties. Single. Unemployed (graduate).	Homelessness (had been a hospital in-patient for most of the past 30 years).	1: client decided not to come in again since we could not provide him with a home.	Unlikely to be helped at Isis Centre.

original problems had pervaded his working, home and personal life with a spirit of unease and dissatisfaction. He had found it hard to focus his attention on any particular area in counselling, and had felt vaguely frustrated by that too. He said that he felt less distressed now, but seemed to have achieved this by means of rather quiescently abandoning hope. This seems to be a kind of resignation that is very different from that described by Jacques as 'constructive'. This man defended against unhappiness by the unemphatic assertion that happiness is not a possibility and so not a loss.

A fourth person took this sequence a step further. He coldly asserted that counselling had been useless for him, and his attitude was cynical and bitter. His experience, within counselling and outside it, was of coldness and futility; his style was chilly but damning. He had been unable to invest any hope in the relationship and his counsellor could not help him.

We go on now to consider the women in our sample who were in the older age-group (Table 11.2). Women aged forty or more form a significant proportion of those who come to the Isis Centre. Of the twenty-three people in this group, one was single; twelve were married; ten were divorced or widowed. All but three had children, many of whom had grown up and either had left home or were soon to do so. There were eleven women with professional occupations, including six teachers; there were three housewives, five people in unskilled work, and three who were unemployed. Their ages ranged from forty to sixty-three.

Only four of these women had no previous experience of help of any kind for their emotional difficulties. Nine had had hospital treatment, six as inpatients. Seven others relied heavily on their general practitioners; three had also been to marriage guidance; three had been in individual therapy.

Their pattern of attendance at the Isis Centre curiously resembles that of the young men. That is, there is a clear separation into those who came once only, and those who settled to work, in some of these cases staying for a very long time indeed. Although there is some overlap, it is generally true to say that the prevailing feelings of those who came for a series of sessions were depression and anger, grief and rage; those who came only once were more usually characterised by acute anxiety, often focused on someone else.

Of the nine women of this age who came only once, eight were married and living with their husbands and children. In all but two cases, their anxieties concerned other members of the family. They were focused, for example, on a teenage son or daughter, and they were often compounded by disagreements with the husband as to the management of the family problem.

In several instances the single consultation seemed to serve a useful

TABLE 11.2 Women: aged forty years and over.

Total sample: 144, of whom 91 were women
of these, 23 were forty or more
i.e. 25 per cent

Average number of sessions: 21   Range: 1–136 (+ one still continuing)

Ref. no., age, marital status and occupation	Problems	Number of sessions	Outcome
		(Information from clients' accounts)	
(104) 48 years. Divorced (four children, 30, 28 25 and 18 years). Unemployed (later part-time shop assistant).	Depression; end of a relationship with a man friend; housing and financial problems; physical illness; eating phobia.	69: open-ended work – weekly at first, later moving to fortnightly. Two series: 46 + 23. Terminated when client left Oxford.	Client wrote very positively of her experience and detailed many areas of beneficial change – in feelings, symptoms and relationships. (Follow-up questionnaire.)
(105) 47 years. Married (two children, 11 and 10 years). Artist and part-time teacher.	Marital problems.	5: four evaluative and a review. Client then chose to stop.	No longer depressed. Thinking energetically and constructively – taking a different attitude to the problems in her marriage. Used the sessions to start off vigorously in a new direction. (Follow-up interview.)

151

TABLE 11.2 – CONTINUED

Ref. no., age, marital status and occupation	Problems	Number of sessions	Outcome
(106) 43 years. Divorced (two children, 14 and 13 years). Teacher.	Break-up of marriage in the previous year: anger and despair. Suicidal impulses.	136: weekly, with one period of coming fortnightly. Client chose when to terminate.	More resigned to unhappiness; less hopeful of happiness. Still angry but able now to contain this, not go out of control. Promotion at work. Still lonely for someone to talk to. (Follow-up interview.)
(107) 48 years. Married (two children, 23 and 21 years). Research worker.	Relationships with her children.	7: open-ended: client chose to stop.	Improvement in relationships with children. Rather reserved about the experience. (Follow-up questionnaire.) (Later returned for further counselling with the same counsellor.)
(108) 51 years. Divorced (three children, 23, 21 and 15 years). Teacher.	Severe anxiety states associated with relationship with teenage daughter. Loneliness.	8: counsellor felt there had been an agreed contract for 12 sessions; client was more vague. *Her* decision to stop.	Improvement in relationship with daughter. More accepting of self – a bit less isolated and coping better. Yet feeling that the good changes are rather precarious. (Follow-up interview.)
(109) 54 years. Divorced (four children, 32, 30, 28 and 19 years). Teacher.	Depression.	19: a series of groups of sessions: 4 + 1, 7 + 6 + 1. Some discrepancies between accounts of termination.	Some increase in confidence and self-respect. Client unsure whether she attributed some recent good changes to counselling or not. Very mixed feelings about it. (Follow-up interview.)

(110) 41 years. Divorced/cohabiting (two children, 17 and 14 years). Unemployed (then student at C.F.E.).	Confusion.	27: open-ended work; end determined by client going on full-time course.	Perhaps 'a little more insight'. Otherwise reserved about the outcome. 'I was unable to let myself go — I was too controlled'. (Follow-up questionnaire.)

No follow-up

(Information from counsellors' accounts)

(111) 43 years. Widowed (one child, 14 years). Paramedical worker.	Rage and grief at suicide of husband; depression; suicidal feelings; difficulty in sustaining relationships.	79: over six years, at fortnightly or longer intervals. Terminated by mutual agreement.	Seemed to re-value herself and recover reason for living. Made new relationships and stopped coming when she decided to get married again. (Not followed up, as she maintains occasional contact with her counsellor.)
(112) 63 years. Divorced. Civil servant.	Depression concerning problems at work.	35: over 5½ years, at fortnightly, monthly or six-weekly intervals. Client's decision to terminate.	Client decided to seek private therapy. Counsellor saw the work as related to retirement problems. He advised against follow-up.
(113) 44 years. Widowed (three children, 22, 17 and 12 years). Cleaner.	Constant worrying; unable to be alone. Fears of psychiatric treatment.	4: three evaluative, then a contract for ten. Client cancelled after the first of these.	Client already had support from G.P. and social worker. Counsellor felt this was probably more appropriate than counselling. Client did not reply to letter requesting a follow-up interview or questionnaire.

TABLE 11.2 – CONTINUED

Ref. no., age, marital status and occupation	Problems	Number of sessions	Outcome
(114) 52 years. Married (one adult son). Housewife.	Husband ill; socially isolated. Physical symptoms and acute anxieties about her health.	5: four evaluative and one review after a month. Client then took up suggestion of psychodrama course – two or three sessions only – and private psychotherapy.	Client decided to go into private therapy. (At follow-up she agreed to an interview but did not come. Did not respond to an offer of another appointment, nor complete a questionnaire that was sent.)
(115) 40 years. Single. Landlady.	Career and family decisions.	29: fortnightly and with many cancellations. Original plan of short-term intervention abandoned as inappropriate – then open-ended work. She cancelled an appointment and made no further contact.	She had got some way towards achieving her goals, e.g. had got a place at a college for further study. She seemed 'more organised, within and without'. (Not followed up, at counsellor's recommendation, as not truly terminated).
(116) 40 years. Married (two children). Part-time teacher.	Fear of harming others. Depression and anger. Relationship difficulties.	32: two series of 15 and 17 sessions, with a ten month gap between.	Counsellor advised against follow-up. Client returned to continuing care of psychiatrist.

Continuing

(117)

Single sessions

(118) 49 years. Married (four children, 26, 22 21 and 17 years).	Depression; exhaustion and lack of concentration at work; marital and family problems.	1: since she lived at a distance and there were appropriate resources nearer to her home.	A useful, exploratory, clarifying session.
(119) Forties. Married (four children, 20, 19, 16 and 13 years). Part-time teacher.	Anxieties about 19 year old son; disagreements with husband. Wanting son to come for help.	1: mutually agreed.	Clarifying what was and was not possible in the way of help; for herself; for her and husband; or for son. Clarification and reassurance.
(120) Forties. Married (children? – unknown). Works for Post Office.	Marital problem, in crisis.	1: a further session was agreed but client phoned to cancel it.	Counsellor felt some issues were clarified.
(121) 45 years? Married (two children, 19 and 17 years). Housewife.	Anxieties about her teenage daughter. Wanting her to come for help.	1: client cancelled second one.	Client used the session effectively to clarify and ventilate her own feelings. (Daughter meanwhile sought help elsewhere.)
(122) Forties. Married (three children). Teacher.	A marital/sexual problem.	1: since she lived at a distance.	Work towards clarifying the problem and demonstrating that help was possible. Then help with finding resources nearer home. Client later rang to say she had done so.

TABLE 11.2 – CONTINUED

Ref. no., age, marital status and occupation	Problems	Number of sessions	Outcome
(123) Forties. Divorced (one adult son). Sales assistant.	Loss of therapist, who had died; feelings of futility.	1: counsellor offered no more sessions as client was already in treatment elsewhere.	No change.
(124) Fifties. Married (three children, 26, 24 and 21 years). Housewife.	Anxieties about son; disagreements with husband.	1: no further sessions offered or sought, as client was hoping for active intervention in son's life.	Perhaps some clarification, and some off-loading of feelings? But client was frustrated as far as her main wish was concerned.
(125) Fifties. Married (one child, 16 years). Part-time job in bookshop.	Anxieties about son; problems with husband.	1: a second appointment was offered; client said she would phone if she wanted it; she did not do so.	Client was seeking advice; declined opportunity to explore feelings further.
(126) 48 years. Married (two children in twenties). Housewife.	Physical symptoms.	1: mutually agreed.	'It seemed to be a bi-lateral agreement that I could not help the client.'

purpose. Two women had travelled considerable distances to the Isis Centre and it would not have been practicable for them to continue to come regularly. Each, however, felt she had clarified her problems, was more hopeful that help was possible, and resolved to seek help nearer her home. Of those who were expressing concern about their adolescent children, some seem to have found the consultation useful, while one particularly did not. Her urgent wish for someone to intervene actively in her son's life was inevitably frustrated, and she was very disappointed and indignant. In such cases the counsellor is entitled only to explore with the client his or her feelings about the person who is causing concern, and the dilemmas which arise: he can work only with the person who has chosen to come.

Of the fourteen women who came for a longer series of sessions, ten were divorced or widowed. Their family circumstances are clearly in contrast with those of the women who came only once. In nine instances, these women were, among other things, coping with their adolescent children on their own. I have said that angry depression was more typical of them than was anxiety, and they expressed their feelings with great force. Their counsellors often found them hard to negotiate with and there were difficulties about termination in many cases. These difficulties were of an opposite kind to those that tended to occur in the youngest group of women, who were liable to stop coming abruptly and without explanation. The older women tended rather to cling to the contact and found it hard to agree to and bear termination. Generally, their problems were associated with lost or broken relationships; they were lonely and isolated, and so they tended to clutch rather desperately at the counselling relationship. It is clear that a particular goal in contacts such as these must be the successful working through of the issues of termination, related as they are to the attainment of 'constructive resignation', both in relation to the past and to the diminishing future.

In some cases something of this kind does seem to have been achieved. One person wrote eloquently of a sense of personal worth being restored, and of shunned, damaged parts of herself being re-integrated. She felt she had received 'lasting help' which continued to stand her in good stead (case 104). Another woman (105) felt able to take up her life again energetically and constructively. She felt released from self-pity and able to make her own way forward, aroused and interested by the problems, rather than overwhelmed by them.

There was, however, also a rather clear example of change achieved by means of bitter resignation, as we saw occurring among the older men. One person said,

'Over the period of coming to the Isis Centre I became much "better". But now I work from a basis of unhappiness, rather than happiness. Maybe this is common to many middle-aged women. I feel some anger at what has happened to my life, but mostly I can contain this. I don't go out of control so easily. *Other people* say it's nice that I've recovered.' (106-F-43)

There were two other women, both in their forties, who seem, in the course of long contacts with their counsellors, to have gradually clarified some new choices for themselves. Each relinquished the counselling relationship at a time when there was a substantial new development in her life. One had achieved a place at a medical school, and the other had decided to re-marry. There is no follow-up information about either of them yet, but it seems clear that they had each made their way to some courageous decisions, involving resolution of many issues from the past.

It seems reasonable to conclude that work with clients, both men and women, at this stage of life is difficult and demanding, but it also has the potential for achieving good changes. The issues more and more concern endings, and this has particularly to be taken into account at termination; nevertheless, successful contacts also sometimes lead to surprising and energetic new beginnings.

Chapter 12

Marital work

So far we have considered the experiences of those who came to the Isis Centre for individual counselling. An appreciable number of people also come specifically for help with problems arising within their marriages. Sometimes one partner presents alone, to explore what is possible and to determine whether joint sessions might seem to be appropriate. Often it is not immediately clear whether the emphasis in the difficulty is personal and individual, or shared within the marriage. The counsellor in this setting responds to what the presenting person is asking for, and relates this, as well as his own interests and skills, to the decision as to whether to proceed individually or to offer joint sessions. Further discussion is, of course, involved between husband and wife, if they are to decide to come together. Sometimes this agreement has already been reached and the partners both come from the beginning, clear that they want to explore their shared problems together.

There were nine couples in the study sample who sought help because of problems in their marriages. In some instances the husband and wife each had some preliminary individual sessions, in others the work was undertaken together from the start. Table 12.1 gives a brief sketch of each contact.

A wide range of ages is represented in this group, which contains people in their twenties through to those in their fifties. One might also say that marriages are exemplified at various stages of development. Marriages, like individuals, go through a series of developmental phases, and it is important to consider the difficulties that arise in the marital relationship in the context of the current developmental tasks in which the whole family is engaged (Pincus and Dare, 1978). It is possible to distinguish the same differences of emphasis that we have seen in the sample as a whole: that is, situations in which maturational difficulties are dominant, in contrast to those in which the relationship suffers as a result of long-standing personality disorders in one or both members of

TABLE 12.1 Marital problems

9 men – i.e. 17 per cent of the men in the sample
9 women – i.e. 10 per cent of the women in the sample

Ref. no., age, marital status and occupation	Problems	Number of sessions	Outcome
		(Information from clients' accounts)	
(127) (M) 38 years. Married. Writer.	Marital problems, depression, and anxiety in wife and self.	44: six sessions alone and 38 with wife. The work was open-ended, terminated by mutual agreement by both clients and counsellor in response to improvement in the marriage.	Improvement in the marital relationship, and confidence that this would be sustained. Personal anxieties unresolved, but client recognised that these had not been the focus of the work. (Follow-up interview.)
(128) (F) 33 years. Married. Lecturer (two children, 4 and 1½ years).	Depression; physical symptoms; marital problems; anxieties about self and husband. Difficulties at work.	53: she came alone at first, weekly for 3 months. Mutual agreement then to joint sessions with husband. Termination as above.	Client spoke very positively about her experience. She reported much more insight into relationships, with husband, with colleagues and generally. Disappearance of physical symptoms. Improvement in and stabilisation of marriage. Greater self-understanding and acceptance. (Follow-up interview.)

(129) (M) 23 years. Married. Medical technician.	Wife's lack of sexual response.	3 + 13: three sessions with a male counsellor; then referred to a female counsellor. Wife came alone for 3 sessions. 10 conjoint sessions: weekly and later, fortnightly.	'A steady improvement, right from the beginning'. Increased communication and understanding. Considerable improvement in sexual difficulty, but not restored quite to original good level. (Follow-up, joint interview.)
(130) (F) 22 years. Married. Receptionist (no children).			

No follow-up

(Information from counsellors' accounts)

(131) (M) 46 years. Married. Printer.	Difficulties in their relationship; and specific problems in husband's behaviour.	19: two series; one of 12 sessions; then 7 more after a break at Christmas. Termination by mutual agreement, but perhaps primarily decided by husband.	There seemed to be good changes, both individually and in the relationship. Less tension; more communication; less disturbed behaviour. Counsellor had some sense that clients were settling rather early for a limited measure of relief. Clients did not reply to either of two follow-up request letters.
(132) (F) Forties. Married. Shop manageress (three children, 19, 16 and 11).			

TABLE 12.1 – CONTINUED

Ref. no., age, marital status and occupation	Problems	Number of sessions	Outcome
(133) (M) Fifties. Married. Local Government Officer.	Difficulties in their relationship; quarrelling; sexual problems.	3 conjoint sessions. Then wife came alone 3 times and husband came alone 4 times. They cancelled further sessions.	Original agreement to work on their relationship broke down. Individual sessions seemed frustrating and unsatisfactory. Clients did not reply to follow-up request letter.
(134) (F) Fifties. Married. Housewife (one child, 11 years).			
(135) (M) 26 years. Married. Journalist.	Depression; marital problems.	34 sessions: 14 individually, followed by 20 joint sessions with wife.	No follow-up information.
(136) (F) 25 years. Married. Teacher (no children).	Marital stress. Physical handicap causing distress and social embarrassment.	62 sessions. 42 individual sessions, open-ended work. Terminated by mutual agreement. (Client subsequently had 20 joint sessions with her husband and another counsellor.	Self-confidence significantly improved. Increased social activities. She seemed to come to terms with her physical handicaps. (No follow-up: client agreed to come for interview but did not keep the appointment. A questionnaire was sent, but neither this nor a further one was completed.)

Single sessions

(137) (M) 40 years. Married. Artist. (138) (F) Twenties. Married. Housewife (baby).	Husband's violent behaviour in their relationship.	1 session. A second was arranged but they did not come. Word from GP that they had left the area.	Unknown.
(139) (M) Thirties. Married. Office representative. (140) (F) Thirties. Married. Housewife (one child, 3 years).	Marital crisis: husband wanted to leave wife for another woman.	Only one session asked for or offered.	Unknown — counsellor felt that their motivation was very uneven: wife trying to hold husband.

Continuing

2 couples: (141 and 142), (143 and 144).

the partnership. The most disturbed marriages are, of course, those in which the maladaptive tendencies in each partner lock together to create a rigid, inflexible system.

An example from one end of the spectrum would be that of a young couple, as yet without children, and presenting with a sexual and communication problem (129 and 130). This was a basically affectionate marriage, early in its development and needing some help in becoming securely established. This type of problem may be contrasted with the distressing effects of the exacerbation and complication of pre-existing personal anxieties and conflicts in each partner, in the course of their living together (e.g. 127 and 128). In this case, motivation was strong and equal, and significant changes were achieved. In another example (133 and 134), the conflicts were so severe and the mutual hostility so great that no alliance was achieved with their counsellor and no satis-factory agreement as to work that could be attempted.

In two instances, the motivation for coming was so uneven between husband and wife that they did not continue beyond a single session. More typically, the work was prolonged and complicated in structure, involving different patterns of conjoint and individual sessions, as seemed appropriate in each case. Two couples who were seen during the study period are currently attending the Centre again, for further work, so no data is available.

Because marital work is focused on a relationship, rather than an individual, its outcome tends, perhaps, towards the extremes. If the motivation of two people is harnessed towards a single end, they are likely to achieve and sustain significant change; if, on the other hand, the motivation of each is in direct opposition to that of the other, or if they are united in opposition to the counsellor, the situation may be immovable. Considerable time, therefore, has to be spent initially in clarifying a mutually acceptable area and style of work. If this can be achieved the potential for useful change is great, and may be beneficial to a whole family.

The principles of marital work in a setting such as this do not differ basically from those of individual counselling. It is still essential to create an accepting, supportive atmosphere, but this is obviously complicated by the necessity for *two* clients, at odds with one another in many respects, to feel equally heard. In each of the cases involved in this follow-up study, it happens that only one counsellor was involved. Sometimes, a male and female counsellor work together with a married couple, to increase the sense of equal support and attention, and to provide another opportunity of observing the interaction in the sessions. Such interaction, between husband and wife, and between them as individuals and as a couple with their counsellor or counsellors, provides the focus of attention in the session. Attempts are made to understand this in relation to the individual personalities and histories of the clients concerned. The counsellor's role is to observe the processes at work in the session, both as they are enacted before him and in terms of their impact on himself. Reflecting upon rather than acting on his own feelings, he has additional important information about the nature of the relationship between his clients. This dispassionate observation of events both within and without is described by Dicks (1967) as 'objectivity in the presence of involvement'.

In a recent paper, Skynner (1980) reviews current developments in marital therapy. He draws together perspectives from analytic, systems theory and behavioural approaches, and underlines some basic principles. He is emphatic about the value of patient, attentive listening, on the part of the counsellor, and of resistance to the impulse to act in response to the anxiety aroused. Relative stillness on the part of the counsellor helps to keep responsibility in the clients' hands and conveys the confidence that they can manage it. The counsellor thus retains his freedom to assist in the observation and clarification of the difficulties in the relationship, drawing attention to details, both presented and significantly omitted, and to their meanings. Skynner observes that, in offering help to a marriage, 'we are dealing with a unit large enough to possess adaptive and self-corrective therapeutic powers of its own which, if facilitated by the therapist, will ultimately simplify his task and do much of the healing work for him'. As the small sample of cases reported here shows, however, constructive change can only occur if some initial work establishes that it is genuinely the shared desire of the partners that it should do so.

Chapter 13

Discussion

> 'His name was never in the paper. He's not the finest character that ever lived. But he's a human being, and a terrible thing is happening to him. So attention must be paid. . . . Attention, attention must finally be paid to such a person.'
>
> (Arthur Miller, *Death of a Salesman, Act 1*)

My theme has been the urgent necessity of paying serious attention to the distress that is part of the experience, in acute or chronic forms, of so many people. As a society we have become efficient to a very considerable degree in the prevention and treatment of physical disease; our skills lag behind in the care of people suffering from mental pain. Here I am referring not to grief, regret or fear, experienced appropriately in relation to truly sad and fearful events, within oneself or in the outside world. The capacity to experience such feelings, as well as those of joy and anger, is a fundamental characteristic of mental health. I am speaking of the elaborations of depression and anxiety, inappropriate guilt and misplaced aggression, which the self constructs in desperate efforts to avoid or diminish pain. These attempts are part of a retreat from, rather than a recognition of reality, and the temporary relief they afford is precarious. It is when such defensive measures begin to lose their efficacy that people feel the need for some help, and it is with responding to this need that we are concerned. The type of help offered is envisaged not as a means of muffling mental pain, as a drug might do, but as providing a way of managing and thinking about it, so that it can be contained and understood. The goal is not that the distress should be reduced to what seems to be manageable within the troubled person's diminished resources, but that his resources should become more available to him, so that he can understand and cope more directly with his distress.

I have described the development of the Isis Centre, as a resource designed to undertake work of this kind, and also a research study within that setting. This study was of an exploratory kind, seeking to observe the work as it proceeded, and to increase our understanding of what it means to the people who come to the Centre. Its findings illustrate possibilities, rather than establish certainties. They especially underline the need for flexibility and sensitivity in the therapeutic work in a setting to which such a variety of troubled people come. It is clear that beneficial change of a profound and lasting kind can be achieved, but that there are many pitfalls. If ways cannot be found over, around or through such obstacles, clients may suffer increased confusion and despair. The clients' accounts of apparently successful interventions provide valuable clues to methods of overcoming the difficulties inherent in the undertaking. These accounts have been considered both as illustrations of particular, individual experiences, and as they relate to patterns discernible in the common experience of men and women at specific stages in their lives.

Relation of the findings to the original aims of the Centre

In the opening chapter, I described the way in which the Centre was set up, with considerable openness as to how it might evolve. Crucial factors were considered to be that it should offer a meaningful service directly to those who felt they needed it and that it should overlap as little as possible with the work of other resources in the area.

As far as the use made of the Centre is concerned, it achieves the former of these aims. Over the years it has been used steadily, and at present it has the doubtful privilege of having a waiting-list of prospective clients. This may be regarded as an indicator of the pressing need for such resources, but it is at odds with the principle of offering help as near as possible to the time that a person seeks it. We have heard from people in the study that ease of access to the Centre, and the directness of its response, are valued aspects of what it has to offer. Paradoxically, its existence and its accessibility are sometimes cited, particularly by people who have had some experience of counselling there, as reasons for their *not* having to come. The knowledge that it is there seems to provide a supportive background to their efforts to manage for themselves. Similarly, it is possible that professional people in the community, who, without the availability of this sort of resource, might otherwise make rapid formal referrals to hospital services, actually more readily keep and contain within their own care the troubled people who come to them. They thus extend the model exemplified by the Isis Centre, and are supported by its being there if necessary, for consultation, or to offer further counselling to their clients.

As far as the second point is concerned, that of trying not to overlap with existing services, the situation is more complicated. Of the people in the study sample, 35 per cent had experience of previous psychiatric treatment, in a hospital setting. This is consistent with annual figures, which regularly show that between 30 and 40 per cent of our clients have had prior psychiatric care. A further 39 per cent of the people in the study said they had talked seriously about their emotional difficulties with someone before: they had turned to their doctors, health visitors, or social workers; had consulted Marriage Guidance, or other counsellors; or the Samaritans; or they had sought private individual or group therapy. Only 26 per cent of the study sample had not sought help of any kind before.

Overlap in the population served does not, of course, necessarily imply overlap in the work undertaken. In other words, resources such as the Isis Centre can offer help of a different kind to people who cannot make use of the formal medical services, or who, from experience, judge those services to be inappropriate to their needs.

We have seen that previous hospital contact seems to have different implications for different groups of people. It is one of the factors that varies most clearly in relation to the sex and age of the client. The groups with the highest frequency of previous hospital treatment were the older men (66 per cent) and the youngest women (47 per cent). In the former group, this factor was often associated with chronic, intransigent problems and was a poor indicator for useful work at the Isis Centre. In the latter group it was linked to a demanding, expressive style, and may, in many instances, have illustrated the degree of anxiety and concern caused in others by these young women, rather than the intrinsic complexity of their problems. In their case, the fickleness shown in their use of resources was a problem to be dealt with in its own right. In other groups, for example that composed of women trying to recover from the break-down of their marriages, there was also an appreciable rate of previous hospital contact (38 per cent). In this case, this indicated the acuteness of their distress, and the concern with which it was viewed by others. However, that energetic distress seemed also to be one of the factors which led them to make effective use of the Isis Centre.

It seems to be realistic to say that, in some cases, work is undertaken at the Isis Centre which resembles that previously attempted elsewhere, with the same client. Hope then rests with the special structure of the work here; with the particular provision of security and adequate time, accompanied by a high expectation of individual responsibility; and with the facilitating effects of a new beginning in a new setting, even if the tasks are familiar and the difficulties deeply entrenched.

In other cases, especially where the person has no prior experience of formal help of any kind, or in instances where the client is consciously choosing a different approach to his problems, the Isis Centre may be said to be offering a clear addition to existing possibilities. For some groups, as, for example, the younger men, who seemed to have neither sought nor attracted concern and help hitherto, it may be that the special conditions of confidentiality and unobtrusiveness are necessary for them to make an approach at all.

An important question is, of course, whether attendance at the Isis Centre reduces the likelihood of people needing other National Health resources in the future. We can report, on the basis of this study, only on the six months immediately after the end of Isis Centre sessions, and this is a very short time. Nevertheless, it is worth considering what we know. Table 13.1 shows the use of resources, directly related to mental distress, of the 52 people who gave us follow-up information. Many people had, of course, sought help from more than one agency. The information is drawn from answers to the following questions:

'Had you already sought help elsewhere for the problems that you brought to the Isis Centre? If so, from whom?'
'Had you any experience of psychiatric treatment, or any kind of psychological help, before you came to the Isis Centre?'
'Have you sought further help of any kind since your sessions finished at the Isis Centre?'

It must be stressed that the figures in the second column of the table refer to a much shorter period of time than those in the first, and so, at best, they only suggest a possibility of change in the use of resources. If we look in a little more detail, we find that some of the further help-seeking that occurred after sessions at the Isis Centre was directly due to decisions reached by the counsellor and client together. This is true of each of the referrals for psychiatric outpatient treatment. In one case it was felt that the client would benefit from a day-patient programme, for further help for her agoraphobia; in another, the client went on, after the birth of her baby, to a desensitisation programme in relation to her anxiety attacks. The third client consulted with his counsellor before seeking advice from a psychiatrist concerning persistent depression. The five people who went on into therapy groups at the Isis Centre or privately, or into private psychotherapy or analysis, all viewed this, at follow-up, as one of the useful outcomes of their counselling. They may be contrasted with those clients who reported that they had, at some time in the six months since their counselling ended, used some tranquillising or antidepressant medication from their doctors: these clients were regretful that this had still seemed necessary.

Longer-term evidence would be needed to make the case that counselling has a preventive effect as far as further disorder is concerned, and so relieves other resources. The short-term evidence is, however, promising. Another facet of the work is sometimes to put a person in touch with another relevant agency and to facilitate his

TABLE 13.1 Use of resources

Resource	Before this Isis Centre attendance	In six months since this Isis Centre attendance
National Health:		
Hospital: as in-patient	8	0
as out-patient	10	3
GP: medication	17	8
advice	12	3
Isis Centre: individual counselling	2	0
therapy group	0	1
Family Planning Association	2	0
Social Services	2	0
University Counselling Service	4	0
Marriage guidance	7	0
Private therapy: group	0	2
individual	7	2
Co-counselling	1	0
Self-help groups	0	2
Acupuncture	1	1
Samaritans	4	1
None	5	30

approach to it, both emotionally and practically. It should be emphasised that responsible use of appropriate help, at the Isis Centre or elsewhere, is indeed preferable to chronic distress, endured in the belief either that no help is possible or that one is not entitled to it or worthy of it. We have seen some evidence of an increase in a person's self-esteem leading to his being more open to both giving and receiving help.

Relation of the findings to the theories and expectations of the counsellors

One expects in such a study to find some convictions confirmed, some disputed, others perhaps disregarded. Another outcome may be to find a belief so emphatically confirmed that one's earlier grasp of it seems quite inadequate. This is the case here when one considers the emphasis placed by clients on their feelings. Again and again, they describe their feelings as the dominant aspect of their problems; as the decisive factor in their choosing when to seek help; as an essential part of their experience in counselling; and as an area of significant change in the outcome. Even if one, as a counsellor, might say that one already knew this, the consistent emphasis that it carries is very impressive. 'Understanding the client's problem' becomes synonymous with accurately hearing his feelings, facilitating their expression, and participating in disentangling them and clarifying their origins. This is an area for both empathy and analysis, using the resources of both psycho-dynamic theory and the counselling relationship. There can be no doubt that the basic request is generally not: 'Help me solve my problems', but 'Help me understand and manage my feelings, so that I may solve my problems myself'.

In Chapter 2 I outlined some of the ideas fundamental to the work of the Isis Centre. I stressed the importance of the relationship between the counsellor and the client, both as the 'facilitating environment', to use Winnicott's term (1965), and as part of the material to be studied. Clients, likewise, were emphatic about the essential qualities of this relationship, and their need to be able to trust it totally, while still grappling with the feelings, both positive and negative, arising within it.

That negative feelings do arise is amply illustrated, and it is clear that the counselling situation is at once supportive and frustrating. This is one of the many features that it shares with the relationship between parent and child. It shares with that relationship, also, two possibilities: the inevitable frustrations and limitations may either form themselves into an insuperable barrier to development, or they may provide the motive power that successful maturation requires. Here again the clients' reports encourage the counsellor to take the relationship seriously, both intellectually and imaginatively. This requires the most sensitive understanding of the dilemmas involved and the feelings aroused. Clients report that these feelings are very strong but that they are also the most difficult ones to put into words. Much of the counsellor's skill lies in making possible the expression of such emotions, in receiving them and reflecting on them with the client.

Some, then, of our preconceptions seem to have been confirmed. Bowlby's formulation of the process of psychotherapy as beginning with the provision of 'a safe base from which to explore' (Bowlby, 1979) is amply illustrated in the clients' descriptions. Where work did not get successfully under way, it seems often to have been precisely because of the felt absence of these essential conditions of trust and security.

Beyond that, however, there are very conflicting opinions about other aspects of the work, in terms particularly of its structure and its content. As will have been clear from the tables of case outlines, a

171

great variety of patterns of sessions occurred. Some were designed in discussion between counsellor and client, and others were determined by the time available before, for example, the client's leaving the country or having a baby. In other situations again, the counsellor seems to have decided on an appropriate length of time and offered this to the client, as the basis of their working contract. In some instances, of course, termination was abruptly determined by the client's un-explained departure. We find voices expressing both positive and negative views concerning each of the varieties of planned structures.

Some people working in an open-ended way, for example, found this an invaluable expression of the counsellor's attitude of uncon-ditional acceptance. This permitted the gradual development in the client of a sense of readiness to stop, as one expression of his increased independence. Others working in this way became uneasy, feeling that they were filling the time but becoming doubtful as to the necessity of further sessions. People, on the other hand, who worked within time-limited agreements also describe a range of reactions. Some felt an invigorating sense of urgency as a result of their awareness of the inevitability of termination. They made use of this to support their courage in naming and tackling difficult problems. Others, however, working within a similar system, became anxiously preoccupied with it, and felt unable to put much weight on what was so clearly a temporary structure.

Similarly, contrasting opinions are found about the nature of each individual session. Some people spoke warmly of the freedom offered to bring whatever material they wished and to range widely in both presenting and reflecting on it. Others had been unnerved by this openness and unable to make use of it. Others again had experienced their counsellors as actively guiding and focusing the sessions, and had appreciated the feeling of security and purposefulness that this afforded. A few clients, however, had felt pressed to consider areas of their lives and experiences of which they could not see the relevance, and so they were resentful of the restrictiveness of their counsellor's efforts.

Two main themes emerge from these contrasts. One is that it is vital that the client's negative reactions to such aspects of his experience form part of the discussion with his counsellor, rather than being endured alone, without being clarified or explored. The other is the great need for flexibility of approach on the part of the counsellor. If he relentlessly pursues his own theoretical goals, by his own preferred methods, he will inevitably confuse and frustrate an appreciable number of his clients. This process is at least wasteful and may be damaging. If he can be attuned, however, to the needs and feelings of each individual client, he is in a position to design an experience that is likely to be helpful. The findings of this study suggest that relevant judgments may be made not only in the light of factors associated with the personality style of the client and his specific history, but also with regard to common social and cultural factors, related to life-stage and situation. Harry Guntrip emphasises the need to appreciate both the common and the unique features of any person's experience:

> If every patient is ultimately unique in his individuality, it is also true that every patient shares in our basic constitutional heritage as human beings. All human beings have fundamental things in common. We can come across the same kinds of conflicts, of emotional disturbance, of defensive symptomatology, in patient after patient, even though in each separate patient these have an individual nuance. We can pool and sift our knowledge of these experiences so that we can obtain a constantly corrected and expanded body of information about the common stages of human development and how these can be disturbed and distorted. But we can only apply this to any given individual under the guidance of our own intuitive understanding of what is going on at this moment in this patient. (Guntrip, 1971)

A new tradition

The counselling setting I have been describing is in many ways new. The people who come have not been selected according to any expert diagnosis as to their condition, nor by any sophisticated technique for predicting the likely outcome of work of a psychotherapeutic kind. They come because they are troubled, and because they have an inkling or a conviction that they need to understand themselves better. It seems that counsellors in such a setting must undertake to develop a tradition of their own, that blends some strands from other settings and styles of working. The two principle lines of inheritance are from non-directive counselling, and from the study of psychodynamics, as derived from psychoanalysis.

Some certainties that we are entitled to extract from what our clients have told us concern the nature of the relationship that permits useful change to occur. The concepts first formulated by Rogers (1957), of empathic understanding and unconditional positive regard, are illustrated vividly in clients' accounts of factors that they found helpful. These factors have been further studied and refined in the work of investigators such as Truax and Carkhuff, (1967), who define the core ingredients for therapeutic change as 'accurate empathy, non-possessive warmth and genuineness'.

A study which, like our own, produced strong evidence in support of this line of thinking was that reported by Strupp and his colleagues (Strupp *et al.*, 1969). Psychotherapy patients from an outpatient clinic in America reviewed their experiences in therapy. The researchers concluded: 'A sense of mutual trust was unquestionably a sine qua non for successful psychotherapy; in its absence, little of positive value was accomplished.' What they describe as a 'warmth factor' was outweighed in importance only by the quality of respect shown by the therapist for the patient. They had no doubt that the patient's picture of an ideal therapist was of 'a keenly attentive, interested, benign and concerned listener'.

The departure from a strictly Rogerian style of thought, however, can also be illustrated by this American study. Although the therapist's warmth, acceptance and respect were found to be *necessary* conditions for therapeutic change, they did *not* appear to be *sufficient*. They provide an essential context for a particular kind of learning experience. Strupp describes the outcome of this experience in terms which apply directly to the changes reported by those of our clients who underwent beneficial changes. He speaks of:

> The transformation of what seemed to be mysterious and mystifying symptoms into phenomena with explainable antecedents. The patient came to view his difficulties in the context of his inter-personal relations, and this new understanding was accompanied by the development of techniques for more adaptive, less conflictual and more satisfying ways of relating to others. . . . Feelings of confidence, assurance and mastery replaced helplessness, inadequacy and overwhelming despair. In psychoanalytic terms, the patient's natural tendencies towards synthesis, meaning, organisation, competence and growth supplanted his sense of failure and helplessness. (Strupp *et al.*, 1969)

Strupp not only illustrates changes such as this, but gives convincing evidence of their durability.

We see here the linking up of factors clarified in the study of non-directive counselling with the insights derived from psychoanalysis. Strupp makes reference to the concept of the 'corrective emotional experience', which was formulated by Alexander and French in 1946. Their study at the Chicago Institute of Psychoanalysis was designed to explore ways in which use could be made of psychodynamic principles in the course of interventions much shorter than those customary in traditional psychoanalysis. 'Only by a more flexible use of the therapeutic principles of psychoanalysis, adapted to the individual nature of each individual case, can our therapeutic heritage from Sigmund Freud be made truly useful — not merely for a small group but for society at large.' (Alexander and French, 1946). They were interested in the extension of psychoanalytic principles from the treatment of chronic psychoneuroses, to milder forms, to acute neurotic reactions, and to incipient cases of emotional disturbance.

In studying their cases, they evolved the view that it is not always necessary to seek insight into a person's very early experiences. They recognised the impact of later events, much as we have observed in those cases where we have described the disturbance as very strongly situational in origin. 'Neurotic tendencies lie latent in every person. When anyone is exposed to difficulties beyond his powers of adaptation, these latent tendencies may be called into action and an acute neurotic state develop.' They also stress, as has seemed meaningful in relation to our cases, the maturational dimension, in placing and understanding a person's problem. 'In every neurosis we look for that time in the patient's life when he refused to yield to the ever-changing requirements of the process of maturation, to "grow up". This refusal may take place in almost any phase of life.' Acknowledging the natural tendency towards maturation allows one to conceive of the role of the therapist not only in terms of intervening, as for example by interpretation, direction or advice, but also in terms of facilitating, of assisting a process that is in some ways already trying to take place. Alexander and French observe: 'Just as the healing of a wound is a natural function of the human body, so the integration of new insight is a normal function of the ego.'

Malan (1976) reviews the development of brief psychodynamic interventions since the publication of Alexander and French's book, and he argues for the wider application of the principles involved. The work that he reports from the adult department of the Tavistock Clinic vividly demonstrates the nature of the therapy undertaken, and its effectiveness. He also draws out and discusses the psychodynamic principles on which the work is based, urging their more general incorporation into our culture and thought. (Malan, 1979).

Malan is reporting work with carefully selected patients, and he takes pains to clarify the selection criteria used. In this book we have been looking at a further extension of the application of the same principles. In our case, at the Isis Centre, our clients select themselves. The counsellors must then respond, sensitively and accurately, in exploring with each client what is possible. The techniques must be flexible, and the pace and depth of the work adjusted to the emotional capacities of each client, but the fundamental principles remain the same. The goal is that the client should be able to understand his real feelings and bear to experience them, so that he may exercise conscious choices where he has hitherto been driven by motives of which he is not aware. The method involves his unconditional acceptance by his counsellor, who offers his resources of theoretical and self-knowledge, rooted in intellectual understanding, intuition and empathy. The outcome, as has been illustrated by the experience of a significant number of our clients, can be a reduction of neurotic suffering, and a strengthened capacity for reflection and self-observation, that dramatically enhance the quality of a person's life and relationships.

Appendices

Questionnaire and letter

Appendix I Letter sent to clients when their sessions ended

The Isis Centre,
Little Clarendon Street,
Oxford.

Dear   ,

I am writing to you because of your recent contact with the Isis Centre. The Isis Centre is a new venture and we should like to collect some information from its users as to their impression of the service it provides. This would be helpful both for the Centre itself, and in the design of similar projects elsewhere. We are interested in people's feelings about coming to talk to a counsellor here, what they hoped for and what they found. We should like to know whether this experience was felt to be useful, and, if so, in what ways. We are equally concerned to know about people's reservations or disappointment about what we offer.

In order to discover if it has any lasting effect, we should like to hear from people about six months after their contact with the Centre. If you would be prepared to talk for a short while, in confidence, about your experience here, we should be grateful. You would not see the counsellor you saw when you first came in, and the interview could take place either at the Isis Centre or in your own home, whichever would be more convenient for you. If you are willing to participate in this study, would you kindly write your name below, and an address at which you can be contacted in six months' time, and return the slip to the Isis Centre.

If you would like to participate, but think that circumstances then may make an interview impossible, a questionnaire could be sent to you. Would you please indicate if that is so, and provide an address where a questionnaire would reach you.

The identity of all participants in this study will be concealed. With thanks,

Yours sincerely,

I am willing to participate in this study and can come to the Isis Centre/ be seen in my home (please indicate which you prefer) for a short interview in about six months' time.

address: . . . .   'phone no.: . . . .
. . . .
. . . .   Signed:

I am willing to participate in this study but an interview would be hard to arrange. A questionnaire would reach me at:

. . . .   'phone no.: . . . .
. . . .
. . . .   Signed:

I do not wish to participate in this study.
Comments, if you wish:

Signed:

Appendix II Questions which formed the basis of the follow-up interview or questionnaire

1 What would you say was the main problem troubling you when you first came to the Isis Centre?

2 Were there any other things that troubled you at that time, or that emerged in the course of the sessions?

3 Would you say that your problems then:
   — were of very recent onset (i.e. had begun in the last week or two before you came to the Isis Centre)   . . . . . .

- were of fairly recent onset (i.e. had begun during the last few months before you came to the Isis Centre) ......
- had started within the previous year ......
- were long-standing? ......

(Please tick one)

4 Would you say that your problems then caused you:
- extreme distress ......
- moderate distress ......
- mild distress? ......

(Please tick one)

5 To what degree do you feel your problems then were interfering with your everyday activities and relationships:
- a great deal ......
- moderately ......
- little? ......

(Please tick one)

6 What made you choose that particular time (i.e. when you first came to the Isis Centre) to seek some help?

7 Had you already sought help elsewhere for the problems that brought you to the Isis Centre?
If so, from whom?

8 How was it that you chose to come to the Isis Centre? (e.g. how did you know of it? Whose idea was it that you should come?)

9 (a) What did you hope to accomplish for yourself when you came to the Isis Centre? What sort of things did you hope to change or achieve?

(b) In what way or ways did you hope that the Centre might be able to help you?

10 Was there any particular agreement between you and the counsellor as to what you would try to do?
If so, what did you understand this to be?
Did this change at all in the course of the sessions?

11 Did you agree to have a particular number of sessions, or was it left open, to see how you got on?

12 How did you feel about the way in which your sessions at the Centre came to an end?
Whose decision was it, do you think, that you should stop?
Did you want to have any further contact with the counsellor in the future?
Was this possibility discussed?

13 Did the counsellor suggest, at any stage, that you might seek help somewhere else, or of another kind? (e.g. legal advice; marriage guidance; your doctor; social skills training, etc.)   Yes/No
If yes, please specify, and say how you felt about this. Did you take up the suggestion?

14 What happened in the sessions at the Isis Centre? (e.g. what do you feel you were mainly doing? What part did the counsellor play? What sort of things do you think may have helped you? Were there any things about the sessions that you didn't like or found unhelpful?)

15 Have you experienced any changes, good or bad, that you think may have come about because of your counselling experience? (Consider, perhaps, your feelings about yourself; your feelings about and relationships with other people; your activities; your physical health.)

16 What is your overall impression of your counselling experience?

17 Have you sought further help of any kind since your sessions finished at the Isis Centre?

18 Any further comments:

Appendices

If you are willing, it would be helpful to us if you would kindly fill in the following factual data about yourself:

1   Name:

2   Age:

3   Marital status: single . . . .   separated . . . .
                    married . . . .   divorced . . . .
                    cohabiting . . . .   widowed . . . .

4   Children (please give their sex and ages):

5   Occupation: (If you are a housewife, please also give your husband's occupation):

6   Educational level: (If still studying, please indicate at what level)
left school at leaving age (14/15/16) . . . .
school or C.F.E. to 17/18 . . . .
further training (e.g. teachers' training college, nursing) . . . .
. . . .
university/polytechnic first degree . . . .
university postgraduate course . . . .
professional training (e.g. architect's, solicitor's) . . . .
. . . .

7   Would you briefly describe your living situation: (e.g. do you live alone, or with your parents, with your own family, or with friends, etc.? In your own house or flat, or in a college, hostel, lodgings, etc.?)

8   Had you any experience of psychiatric treatment, or any kind of psychological help, before you came to the Isis Centre?   Yes/No.
If so: when was that?
        what sort of treatment did you have?
        how did you feel about it?
        was it helpful?

Bibliography

Agulnik, P.L., Holroyd, P. and Mandelbrote, B. (1976), 'The Isis Centre: a counselling service within the National Health Service', *British Medical Journal*, vol. 2, pp. 355–7.

Alexander, F. and French, T.M. (1946), *Psychoanalytic Therapy: principles and application*, New York, Ronald Press Co.

Balint, M. (1964), *The Doctor, His Patient and the Illness*, London, Pitman Medical Books.

Balint, E. and Norell, J.S. (eds) (1973), *Six Minutes for the Patient: interactions in general practice consultation*, London, Tavistock Publications.

Bowlby, J. (1979), *The Making and Breaking of Affectional Bonds*, London, Tavistock Publications.

Bransby, E.R. (1974), 'The extent of mental illness in England and Wales', *Health Trends*, London, HMSO.

Brown, G.W. and Harris, T. (1978), *Social Origins of Depression: a study of psychiatric disorder in women*, London, Tavistock Publications.

Caplan, G. (1964), *Principles of Preventive Psychiatry*, New York, Basic Books; London, Tavistock Publications.

Cooper, B., Fry, J. and Kalton, G. (1969), 'A longitudinal study of psychiatric morbidity in a general practice population', *British Journal of Preventive and Social Medicine*, vol. 23, pp. 210–17.

Dicks, H.V. (1967), *Marital Tensions: clinical studies towards a psychological theory of interaction*, London, Routledge & Kegal Paul.

Eliot, G. (1871), *Middlemarch*, Harmondsworth Penguin, 1965.

Erikson, E.H. (1950), *Childhood and Society*, New York, Norton.

Feifel, H. and Eels, J. (1963), 'Patients and therapists assess the same psychotherapy', *Journal of Consulting Psychology*, vol. 27, no. 4, pp. 310–18.

Goldberg, D.P. and Blackwell, B. (1970), 'Psychiatric illness in general practice: a detailed study using a new method of case identification', *British Medical Journal*, vol. 2, pp. 439–43.

Goldberg, D.P. and Huxley, P. (1980), *Mental Illness in the Community:*

the pathway to psychiatric care, London and New York; Tavistock Publications.

Guntrip, H. (1971), *Psychoanalytic Theory, Therapy and the Self*, London, Hogarth Press and New York, Basic Books.

Jacques, E. (1965), 'Death and the mid-life crisis', *International Journal of Psychoanalysis*, vol. 40, pp. 502—16.

Jung, C.G. (1933), 'The aims of psychotherapy', republished in *Modern Man in Search of a Soul*, London, Routledge & Kegan Paul, 1961.

Lazare, A., Eisenthal, S. and Wasserman, L. (1975), 'The customer approach to patient-hood: attending to patient requests in a walk-in clinic', *Archives of General Psychiatry*, vol. 32, pp. 553—8.

Lazare, A., Eisenthal, S., Wasserman, L. and Harford, T.C. (1975), 'Patient requests in a walk-in clinic', *Comprehensive Psychiatry*, vol. 16, no. 5, pp. 467—77.

Levinson, D.J. (1977), 'The mid-life transition: a period in adult psychosocial development', *Psychiatry*, vol. 40, pp. 99—112.

Levinson, D.J. (1978), *The Seasons of a Man's Life*, New York, Alfred A. Knopf.

Llewelyn, S.P. and Hume, W.I. (1979), 'The patient's view of therapy', *British Journal of Medical Psychology*, vol. 52, pp. 29—35.

Malan, D.H. (1976), *The Frontier of Brief Psychotherapy*, New York and London, Plenum Medical Book Co.

Malan, D.H. (1979), *Individual Psychotherapy and the Science of Psychodynamics*, London, Butterworth.

Maluccio, A.N. (1979), *Learning from Clients: interpersonal helping as viewed by clients and social workers*, New York, Free Press.

Marris, P. (1974), *Loss and Change*, London, Routledge & Kegan Paul.

Mayer, J.E. and Timms, N. (1970), *The Client Speaks: working class impressions of casework*, London, Routledge & Kegan Paul.

Mechanic, D. (1968), *Medical Sociology: a selective view*, New York, Free Press.

Miller, A. (1949), *Death of a Salesman*, Harmondsworth, Penguin, 1961.

Monro, M. (1965), 'A contribution to psychiatric epidemiology: a comparative study of neurotic illness', thesis submitted for M.D. degree in psychological medicine, University of Aberdeen.

Parkes, C.M. (1971), 'Psychosocial transitions: a field for study, *Social Science and Medicine*, vol. 5, no. 2, pp. 101—15.

Parkes, C.M. (1972), *Bereavement: studies of grief in adult life*, London, Tavistock Publications.

Pincus, L. and Dare, C. (1978), *Secrets in the Family*, London and Boston, Faber & Faber.

Rogers, C.R. (1951), *Client-centred therapy*, Boston, Houghton Mifflin Co.

Rogers, C.R. (1957), 'The necessary and sufficient conditions of therapeutic personality change', *Journal of Consulting Psychology*, vol. 21, pp. 95—103.

Sainsbury, E. (1975), *Social Work with Families: perceptions of social casework among clients of a family service unit*, London, Routledge & Kegan Paul.

Shaw, P. (1977), 'A study of social problems in a group of young women treated with brief psychotherapy', *British Journal of Medical Psychology*, vol. 50, pp. 155–61.

Shepherd, M., Cooper, B., Brown, A.C., and Kalton, G. (1966), *Psychiatric Illness in General Practice*, London, Oxford University Press.

Sifneos, P.E. (1979), *Short term dynamic psychotherapy: evaluation and technique*, London and New York, Plenum Medical Book Co.

Skynner, A.C.R. (1980), 'Recent developments in marital therapy', *Journal of Family Therapy*, vol. 2, pp. 271–96.

Storr, A. (1960), *The Integrity of the Personality*, Heinemann.

Storr, A. (1979), *The Art of Psychotherapy*, London, Secker & Warburg, and Heinemann.

Straker, M. (1968), 'Brief psychotherapy in an outpatient clinic: evolution and evaluation', *American Journal of Psychiatry*, vol. 124, no. 9, pp. 105–12.

Strupp, H.H., Fox, R.E. and Lessler, K. (1969), *Patients view their psychotherapy*, Baltimore, Johns Hopkins Press.

Szasz, T. (1970), *Ideology and Insanity*, first published in USA 1970; London, Calder & Boyars, 1973.

Taylor, L. and Chave, S. (1964), *Mental Health and Environment*, London, Longman.

Truax, C.B. and Carkhuff, R.R. (1967), *Toward effective Counselling and Psychotherapy*, Chicago, Aldine Press.

Vaillant, G.E. (1977), *Adaptation to Life*, Boston, Toronto, Little, Brown & Co.

Wing, J.K. and Hailey, A.M. (eds) (1972), *Evaluating a community psychiatric service: the Camberwell Register, 1964–1971*, London, Oxford University Press.

Wing, J.K. and Wing, L. (1970), 'Psychotherapy and the National Health Service: an operational study', *British Journal of Psychiatry*, vol. 116, pp. 51–5.

Winnicott, D.W. (1965), *The maturational Processes and the facilitating Environment*, London: Hogarth Press and the Institute of Psychoanalysis.

Wolff, H.H. (1977), 'Loss: a central theme in psychotherapy', *British Journal of Psychology*, vol. 50, pp. 11–19.